1 ου

JOURNEY TO JERUSALEM

DAVID WINTER

JOURNEY TO JERUSALEM

*Bible readings from Ash Wednesday
to Easter Sunday*

Text copyright © David Winter 2007
The author asserts the moral right
to be identified as the author of this work

Published by
The Bible Reading Fellowship
15 The Chambers, Vineyard
Abingdon OX14 3FE
Website: www.brf.org.uk

ISBN 978 1 84101 485 2
First published 2007
10 9 8 7 6 5 4 3 2 1 0
All rights reserved

Acknowledgments
Unless otherwise stated, scripture quotations are taken from The New Revised
Standard Version of the Bible, Anglicized Edition, copyright © 1989, 1995 by the
Division of Christian Education of the National Council of the Churches of Christ in
the USA, and are used by permission. All rights reserved.

New English Bible copyright © 1961, 1970 by Oxford University Press and
Cambridge University Press

Passover text taken from *The Passover Celebration: A Haggadah for the Seder*, ed. Rabbi
Leon Klenicki (Liturgy Training Publications, 1980).

A catalogue record for this book is available from the British Library

Printed in Singapore by Craft Print International Ltd

CONTENTS

Part Three: The destination reached

Part Four: Tragedy—and triumph

INTRODUCTION

It was the 17th year of the reign of the emperor Tiberius—about AD29 in our calendar. He chose to spend many months of the year at his palace on the southern headland of the beautiful island of Capri, overlooking the blue waters swirling below. He probably felt rather pleased with himself. His empire was, relatively speaking, at peace—a peace enforced by a splendid system of law and the most finely trained and equipped (and, when necessary, ruthless) army in human history. From the northern plains of Europe to the Mediterranean sea, and from the wild islands of Britain to the deserts of Arabia and north Africa, Rome ruled.

There had never been an empire quite like this. Its architects and engineers built roads, aqueducts, theatres and arenas. Its lawyers, orators and judges administered the law. Having largely absorbed the culture of Greece, more and more people were educated and sophisticated. The Senate and the tribunes of the people were there, in principle at least, in the interests of a kind of democracy. Yes, Tiberius could justifiably feel that he was ruler of an empire that would last for ever.

As he hunted the wild boar on Capri, far away to the east in a remote and troublesome province of his empire twelve young men were walking with their leader along a road near Caesarea Philippi. They were about 30 miles north of Galilee, in a hilly area where the river Jordan had its source. As they walked, their leader put two questions to them, and the answer to the second one would have profound consequences not just for them but for the future of Tiberius' empire and eventually the whole world.

The leader was Jesus. The twelve young men (and they *were* young, most of them barely in their 20s) were his disciples.

This story begins with those questions and the disciples'

answers to them, and then traces the dramatic and painful consequences of that conversation on the road. The conversation itself would eventually set them on the path to Jerusalem, where the enemies of Jesus were waiting to pounce on the unorthodox young prophet from Galilee. It set in train a sequence of events which we shall see as three acts of a great drama—a drama that encompassed all the fundamental themes of every tragic story and every tale of triumph ever told. It included a quest, as many great stories do, but the quest was not for personal glory, wealth or the hand of a beautiful princess. It was a story of 'rags to riches', as the son of a carpenter from the obscure and sometimes ridiculed village of Nazareth changed the history of the world so profoundly that its most common calendar was to be measured in terms of years before or after his coming. It was a story of opposition overcome, of a dark and malign power to be faced, of tragedy and—ultimately —of triumph. It is the story of Jesus, but it is supremely God's story, the record of an act of rescue on a global scale and with eternal consequences.

It is also, of course, our story—the story that shapes the faith and life of every Christian the world over. With the disciples we experience the awakening of faith in Jesus. With them we hear the challenge to follow him, wherever he leads us. With them we tread the path to Gethsemane and the time of testing, and to Golgotha, the place of crucifixion. With them we find the tomb empty on Easter morning and understand that this journey has no end, only eternal life. It is the story of our baptism, dying with Christ and rising with him to new life. It is the story of our eucharist, as the one who fed the crowds with bread and fish provides food for our spiritual pilgrimage. This Lent we are walking the gospel itself.

It is no exaggeration to say that the journey to Jerusalem of this group of young men (and, later, several women too) would change the world for ever. It could also be claimed that the story of that journey as related to us through the words of the writers of the four Gospels is, as one film epic entitled it, 'The Greatest Story Ever Told'. That story, those events and the group of disciples slowly making their way southwards towards Jerusalem will be the subjects of our Lenten reflection.

The Sunday readings throughout the book will be on the theme of 'following'.

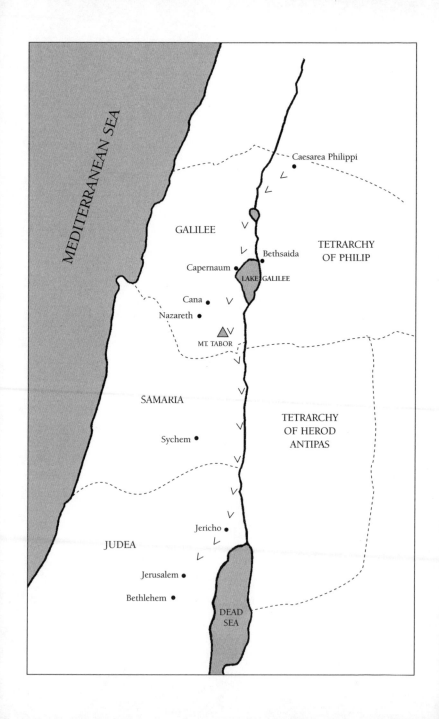

Part One

PREPARING FOR THE JOURNEY

CONFESSION AND COST

READ LUKE 9:18–27.

Key verse: '*Who do you say that I am?*' *(v. 20).*

The little group of twelve men and their leader, whom they called 'Rabbi' (Teacher) or 'Lord', strolled along in the afternoon heat. Possibly someone was laughing about the public's reaction to what they had seen on their travels across Galilee—the healings, the amazing teaching, even the casting out of demons. If that were so, then the first question Jesus put to them simply followed on from the conversation. 'Tell me,' he said, 'who do people say I am?'

At one level that was easy, because all it sought from them was an opinion. 'John the Baptist' was one suggestion—back from the dead, of course, because Herod had had him executed some time previously. 'Elijah,' offered another—the prophet who was expected to appear again before the coming of the Messiah. Even Jeremiah was suggested (see Matthew 16:14), the man who had prophesied the downfall of Jerusalem six centuries earlier. Jesus listened but made no response.

Then he asked a second question. This was a far more difficult one because it was one they had all been thinking about for a long time, and they knew it was the final clue to the whole enterprise that Jesus had called them to join. 'But who do *you* say that I am?'

Perhaps there was silence for a moment as they all looked at each other, wondering if they should put into words the awesome notion that had begun to take root in their minds. Typically, it was Peter who spoke first, expressing that elusive and frightening conviction that they were beginning to share. 'You are the Messiah of God,' he declared.

It's hard for a Christian today, especially one from a Gentile background, to realize the enormity of what Peter had said. From childhood the disciples had learnt that the Lord God is One, so any notion that a human being could share in any way his divinity was genuinely shocking—blasphemous. They had also been taught to pray and look for the coming of the promised Messiah ('Christ' in Greek), God's special and unique representative who would come in the fullness of time to redeem Israel and restore its kingdom— the kingdom of David. For long centuries the Jewish people had waited and prayed for his coming, through days of exile and suffering, through humiliation and slavery and, most recently, through three centuries, no less, of foreign occupation.

There had, it is true, been many who had claimed messiahship, especially in recent years. One after another they would appear, parade the stage for a time and then disappear, sometimes executed by the Romans, sometimes exposed as false by the people's religious teachers and leaders. Possibly, in some quarters, the hope that a true messiah would ever come was fading. After all, John the Baptist had seemed to have all the necessary qualifications, and yet he had strongly refuted the idea that he was the Messiah.

Strangely, he had pointed to another, one who would come after him, whose sandals he wouldn't be worthy to untie. He gave a few of his disciples an even more specific indication. When John baptized Jesus in the river Jordan, he told them, 'Here is the Lamb of God who takes away the sin of the world' (John 1:29). Among the twelve on the road near Caesarea Philippi were at least two of those who had heard his words, whatever they had thought he meant at the time—James and John. As they shared with the others the impact of the words Peter now spoke, they may well have thought of that moment by the banks of the Jordan.

Could it really be that the man with whom they had spent the last two years, hearing him speak, witnessing the healings and other works of power, but also sleeping with him in the open air, seeing him sometimes tired, sweat-stained and hungry, was God's promised one? Could they have spent all those months in the close company of the Messiah? They had probably wondered at times and hoped and longed for certain evidence. Yet now they had, it seemed, collectively made up their minds. Jesus, their friend and leader and teacher, was also the anointed Servant of God, the Son of David and even, in those terrifying words added in Matthew's Gospel, 'the Son of the living God' (16:16).

If, for a moment, doubts and fears arose, it would at least be understandable. After all, John the Baptist himself, who had borne such a clear witness to Jesus at his baptism, later seems to have entertained doubts. He sent some of his disciples to Jesus to ask, 'Are you the one who is to come, or are we to wait for another?' (Luke 7:19). Jesus did not send a 'yes' or 'no' answer, but told them instead to return to John with an account of what they had seen: the sick healed, the lame walking, the blind restored to sight and the poor receiving the good news. Presumably he was confident that John would draw from that evidence the assurance he sought.

The twelve had seen similar sights, of course, over and over again. They can have had no doubt that Jesus was a mighty prophet but, until this moment, even they had held back from any open confession that he was the Messiah of God. Now the words were spoken. What would the reaction of Jesus be?

When it came, it was as unexpected, as unpredictable, as everything else they had heard from him from the moment when he first enlisted them. Mark and Luke simply record that as soon as Peter had spoken, Jesus issued a strict warning that they were not to tell anyone else what they had discovered—the 'messianic secret' that is such a feature especially of Mark's Gospel. He went on to introduce them to a new and disturbing element in his teaching. 'The Son of Man must undergo great suffering and be rejected by the elders, chief priests, and scribes, and be killed, and on the third day be raised' (Luke 9:22).

Jesus then had some stern words for all the crowd—presumably, the people who had been attracted by his earlier teaching or by the miracles of healing and had followed him as he travelled. If they truly wanted to become his followers, he warned, then they would need to 'deny themselves and take up their cross daily and follow' him (v. 23).

'Taking up the cross' seems a clear enough instruction to Christians today: we are to share Christ's sufferings, to be 'crucified with Christ', in the language of Paul. For Jesus' immediate hearers, however, its meaning would have been rather different. They were familiar with the concept of 'carrying the cross' because it was a normal part of the punishment of those who had been sentenced to crucifixion. As one element in the whole degrading process, the condemned person was required to carry the crossbeam on his shoulders to the place of execution. Probably everyone in the crowd, no matter how young, would have seen it happen, because crucifixions at the time were hideously frequent. When Jesus was a boy of about twelve, the Roman general Varus crucified 2000 men and boys alongside the road leading from Nazareth, in retaliation for an uprising against the occupying power. To take up the cross, then, meant to share its humiliation, to shed any notion of superiority or status. Only by 'losing their lives' in this way would they truly find them.

This, Jesus said, was what it would mean for them if they wished to follow him all the way—the way that led inevitably to Jerusalem.

A reflection

As we start our Lenten journey as followers of Jesus, it's probably a good idea to be absolutely clear about the identity of the person we are following. Having walked with Jesus for a couple of years, the disciples were clear about their answer: he was the Messiah of God. That wasn't the end of the learning, any more than there is an end to learning for us—but it's a very good start. Jesus is the one whom God sent to be the Saviour of the world.

Day 2: Thursday

NO EASY WAY

READ MATTHEW 16:21–23.

Key verse: 'You are setting your mind not on divine things but on human things' (v. 23).

After Peter had put into words the disciples' answer to the question of Jesus ('Who do you say that I am?'), he was congratulated by Jesus: 'Blessed are you, Simon son of Jonah! For flesh and blood has not revealed this to you, but my Father in heaven' (v. 17). He was then rewarded with a new name, 'Peter'—*Petros* in Greek, 'a rock'—and he was told that the whole Church of Christ in the future would be built on the rock-like foundation of his confession (vv. 18–19). From what we learn of Peter in the Gospels, this commendation would have boosted his confidence, perhaps to a dangerous degree. At any rate, when he heard the words of Jesus warning them about his suffering and death, which lay ahead in Jerusalem, the Rock-Man decided it was time to put the Messiah right. He took Jesus aside and began to rebuke him: 'This must never happen to you' (v. 22).

In turn, Jesus rebuked Peter. Indeed, he called him Satan, which means 'adversary'. If Peter was opposing this declaration of future suffering, he was opposing everything that the Messiah had come to do. To confess that Jesus was the Messiah, as Peter (and, by inference, all of them) had just done, also required them to accept Jesus' authority. Yet here was Peter, the words of faith barely off his lips, challenging and daring to correct that authority: 'God forbid it, Lord!' The very phrase includes a contradiction.

Peter's fundamental error, Jesus said, was not simply one of misunderstanding his words. It went much deeper than that. When he confessed Jesus as Messiah (and as 'Son of the living God'), he was speaking as the recipient of a divine revelation. It was God, the 'Father in heaven', who had revealed this profound truth to him. Now, in opposing what Jesus knew to be his Father's purposes, he had put himself on a collision course with the will of God, which is not a good or safe place to be. He was now the voice of what we might call the opposition.

Peter's chief fault was not in his intentions but in his thinking. That's what the words of Jesus imply: 'You are setting your *mind* not on divine things but on human things.' Whereas, a few minutes earlier, his mind had been tuned to the will of God, now he was reacting simply as a human being faced with a disturbing problem. He didn't like what he was hearing from Jesus. It ran counter to his expectations and hopes. It involved pain and suffering and death for someone he loved and admired and had just confessed to be the Messiah of God. There must be some mistake!

In fact, all of us need several conversions: conversion to belief in the living God, conversion to belief in Jesus as Saviour, conversion of will, by which we seek to do what God requires rather than what we want, and also conversion of thinking. That is the precise meaning of the word 'repentance', which Jesus constantly set out as a precondition of faith in him: 'repent and believe'. The Greek word translated 'repentance' is *metanoia*, which simply means 'mind-change'. It was here that Peter, like so many of us, hit a problem.

The apostle Paul has quite a bit to say about this. In his letter to the Romans he refers to it explicitly. Negatively, wrong thinking led the ungodly into spiritual darkness: 'they became futile in their thinking, and their senseless minds were darkened. Claiming to be wise, they became fools' (Romans 1:21–22). Positively, right thinking leads to spiritual light: 'be transformed by the renewing of your minds, so that you may discern what is the will of God—what is good and acceptable and perfect' (12:2). In both cases, the clue lies in their thinking. Wrong thinking leads to wrong decisions, and wrong decisions lead to wrong actions. Most of us would probably admit that, although we like to feel that our thinking is in line with our confessed faith, too often we find them in conflict—as Peter did here.

His 'wrong thinking' was about the Messiah. He had confessed that Jesus was the Messiah of God, yet his thinking showed a very limited vision of what that messiahship entailed. Most Jews of the time had a clear picture in their minds of what the coming of God's Messiah would bring about. Like a latter-day Moses or Joshua, he would deliver the people from subjugation to Gentile rule and bring them into the 'promised land'. Not only would the Messiah restore the kingdom of David, but he would also occupy his throne. Already, as we shall soon see, the disciples were mentally allocating to themselves the posts of power in the coming kingdom of Jesus.

This, however, was human thinking, not divine. Jesus was very clear about what being God's Messiah entailed, and it was a million miles from the popular model. Far from coming to conquer, he had come to suffer. Far from allocating posts of worldly power, he would call his followers to suffering, self-sacrifice and loving service—and set the supreme example himself. He would be the true Messiah, but a Messiah who was the suffering servant of Yahweh spoken of in Isaiah, a Saviour who would be wounded, crushed and bruised for his people. Upon him the Lord God would lay their iniquity as if he were a sacrificial lamb. He would bear their punishment and, by doing so, 'make them whole' (Isaiah 52:13—53:12). Those who confessed Jesus as Messiah would have to accept that this was the model he was following. It would be a painful lesson to swallow, and it would occupy the whole journey to Jerusalem and beyond before it was fully learnt.

A reflection

There is no easy way to follow a Saviour who obediently trod the path of self-sacrifice, yet that very path has proved to many to be a way of joy and light.

Day 3: Friday

DISCIPLES AND SHEPHERDS

READ MATTHEW 9:36—10:1.

Key verse: [Jesus] saw the crowds... were harassed and helpless, like sheep without a shepherd (v. 36).

It's time to look a little more closely at the twelve men who confessed Jesus to be the Messiah and committed themselves to following him. Who were they, what was their background and to what task or ministry was Jesus calling them?

So far as we can tell, they were all Galileans except (significantly, perhaps) Judas Iscariot. Galilee was separated from Jerusalem and Judea by the wilderness and the land of Samaria. For geographical and historical reasons, that separation was important because it meant that the Galileans, while certainly Jewish, were not moulded by the temple culture of Jerusalem. Indeed, as a reference in Isaiah expresses it, many people in Jerusalem called the area 'Galilee of the Gentiles', as it was felt to be unduly influenced by the non-Jewish cultures around it.

Galileans were independent, rural, hardworking and mostly poor. They had a distinctive accent—certainly as distinctive as a Yorkshireman would sound in a London street. They cultivated their vines, olives and other crops and those who lived near the lake of Galilee made their living (as at least four of the disciples did) from fishing. The little towns of Galilee are familiar to us from the Gospels: Capernaum (which seems to have been the base for much of the ministry of Jesus), Cana, Nazareth, Bethsaida, Nain,

Chorazin and Tiberias. Across the lake to the east was the land of the Gadarenes, to the north Caesarea Philippi and Tyre, and to the south Samaria and then Judea. The distances involved were not vast—60 miles or so from Nazareth to Jerusalem—but long enough to deter casual travel on foot.

Still, the Galileans made regular pilgrimages to the capital for the great temple feasts, as Jesus did with his family as a boy (Luke 2:41–50). We find in the Gospels that there were travellers in the opposite direction, too. The scribes and Pharisees came up from Jerusalem to make a judgment about the young prophet from Galilee, Jesus of Nazareth, and were not impressed by what they saw (Matthew 15:1–2).

So the men Jesus chose as his disciples (the word simply means 'learners'—they were to sit at his feet to absorb his teaching and to follow his example) were a fairly ordinary cross-section of humanity. As well as the fishermen, there was a former tax collector (not a poor man!), a reformed member of a liberation movement (the 'Zealots'—Luke 6:15), and Judas Iscariot, always and ominously listed as 'the one who betrayed him'. This assorted band was chosen by Jesus after a night of prayer and, with the obvious exception of Judas, proved in the end to be worthy apostles, or 'messengers' of Jesus. Many, if not most, of them lost their lives eventually through their faithful confession of the risen Lord.

It's worth remembering that few would have had anything more than a rudimentary education, learning enough to be able to read the scriptures at their bar mitzvah ceremonies but some way short of what we might today consider necessary qualifications for the sole trustees of the gospel of Jesus. They are living proof of the power of God to take what the world regards as weak and foolish and use it to turn its tawdry standards upside down. The apostle Paul put it in trenchant language in his first letter to the Corinthians: 'not many of you were wise by human standards, not many were powerful, not many were of noble birth. But God chose what is foolish in the world to shame the wise; God chose what is weak in the world to shame the strong; God chose what is low and despised in the world, things that are not, to reduce to nothing things that are, so that no one may boast in the presence of God' (1:26–29). The disciple-apostles, having sat at the feet of Jesus, were able to confound rulers, establish the Christian Church on sound foundations, preach the gospel message to people of many different cultures and—directly or indirectly—help to create the amazing collection of documents that make up our New Testament.

Immediately, however, Jesus saw them as shepherds and evangelists, as our passage makes clear. He had compassion on 'the crowds', the hordes of people who flocked to hear him, desperate for a message of hope, confused and overwhelmed by the pressures of everyday life. Like most of us, they were looking for direction, for someone to show them the way. It was the desperate need he saw in their eyes that moved him: the phrase translated 'had compassion' literally means stomach-churning. Jesus compared them to 'sheep without a shepherd', and here was the 'good shepherd', Jesus himself (John 10:14), longing to meet their need. One way to achieve this was to appoint 'under-shepherds', and he evidently thought of the Twelve as filling that role. They would share his compassion, bring his message of hope to the crowds and even share his ministry of healing (Matthew 10:1).

They would also be evangelists in the sense that there was a harvest to be gathered in—a human harvest simply waiting to be reaped but still untouched because there were too few labourers to do the work. Jesus saw the need and had the wisdom to know that he couldn't reach all of these people on his own. Here were the men who could share the task with him—the immediate task he had set himself of proclaiming the kingdom of God to the 'lost sheep of the house of Israel' (Matthew 10:6).

I have said that the disciples were a fairly ordinary cross-section of humanity, which is true, but that doesn't mean that they were socially or characteristically identical to each other. Some of the group remain quite anonymous in the Gospel records, but we can easily detect personal traits in a number of them. James and John, for instance, were nicknamed 'Sons of Thunder', so clearly they were men of strong views strongly expressed. They were also rather ambitious, because no sooner had Jesus begun to talk about his kingdom than they were at his side getting in their early bids for the places of honour (see, for example, Mark 10:35–40). It is quite amusing that, in Matthew's parallel account (20:21–23), it is their mother who comes seeking preferment for her boys. John, of course, is generally reckoned to be the mysterious 'beloved disciple' of the fourth Gospel. If that magnificent book is in any way the product of his reflection and thought, then it must rank as one of the wonders of the world, coming from a man who started life as a rather fiery fisherman on Galilee. The book operates at many different levels of understanding and interpretation, with literary and theological subtleties that have kept scholars busy for 20 centuries. It is, at the very least, a lasting testimony to the transforming effect that Jesus of Nazareth had on his closest followers.

Then there is Peter—the impetuous, talkative, eager leader of the group. He could 'talk the talk' long before he learned to 'walk the walk', but that's not such a rare experience, as many of us have painfully found out. He was always quick to answer or respond to an invitation, even climbing out of the boat in a storm on Galilee to join Jesus walking on the water (Matthew 14:28–30). Typically, of course, he lost his nerve when he saw the waves. More seriously, he swore adamantly that, although all the other disciples might desert Jesus, he would never in any circumstances, even the threat of death, deny him (John 13:37)—only to do precisely that in the courtyard of the high priest's house later the same night (18:25–27).

Thomas and Philip are also recognizable characters in the apostolic band. Thomas had a restless intellect, compelled to ask the awkward question or play the sceptic in any situation. Thus he questioned Jesus' claim that they 'knew the way' to the Father (John 14:5) and later famously insisted on visual and tangible evidence for the resurrection of Jesus (20:24–25). Many of us can relate to so-called 'doubting Thomas', although in truth it wasn't so much doubt that he expressed as a longing for his faith in Jesus to be vindicated. Philip sounds delightfully direct in his approach to such questions: 'Lord, show us the Father, and we will be satisfied' (14:8). Of course they would! All through history people have longed to see God, but it is not possible on earth, even for patriarchs like Moses. In any case, it was really a question of faith in Jesus, as his response to the request showed: 'Have I been with you all this time, Philip, and you still do not know me? Whoever has seen me has seen the Father' (v. 9).

James, John, Peter, Philip, Thomas—it was men like these, a proper mixture of characters and personalities, who made up the 'Twelve'.

The fact that they were all men troubles some readers today, who wonder why Jesus (who went out of his way to affirm the value and status of women) didn't appoint at least one or two female apostles. In terms of first-century culture, the suggestion would have been totally impractical. If the object of the exercise was to proclaim a message and eventually build a new community, only male preachers and male leaders could possibly have done it. Neither men nor women would have taken seriously the testimony or leadership of a female apostle. The marvel is that, in this new community, women were affirmed in a way that they had never been before, so that the missionary apostle Paul could say, 'There is no longer male and female; for all of you are one in Christ' (Galatians 3:28). The body of Christ, the Church, recognizes no distinctions of race, culture or gender. We can and should honour the men Jesus chose as his apostles, who at enormous personal cost 'took up the cross' to follow him, without drawing from that choice the conclusion that *only* men could ever serve him in this or any other way.

The Twelve, as they became known (matching the twelve traditional tribes of Israel in number), were the inner core of a larger band of male and female disciples—possibly at one time running into several hundred people, but shrinking to 120 after the crucifixion and resurrection (Acts 1:15). Humanly speaking, the entire divine plan of redemption hinged on their reliability and faithfulness. As we shall see, the Twelve were not all cut out to be heroes, not all constantly courageous, not all immune to temptations of personal gain or power. Yet with them and on their testimony Jesus dared to build his Church—a body so strong that not even 'the gates of Hades' could prevail against it (Matthew 16:18).

A reflection

It's always easier to mix with people like ourselves, who come from the same background, share our interests, speak our language and mirror our lifestyle, but the Church of Christ is not like that. Following the pattern of the first apostolic band, it mixes up different people, with different nationalities, lifestyles, personalities and temperaments, in a wonderful rainbow of faith. This is its strength, not its weakness.

Day 4: Saturday

THE CONFIRMATION

READ LUKE 9:28–36.

Key verse: 'This is my Son, my Chosen; listen to him!' (v. 35)

The Gospel accounts of Peter's dramatic confession of Jesus as Messiah all end with more or less the same words. Jesus tells the disciples that 'some standing here… will not taste death before they see the kingdom of God' (v. 27). The statement would appear to be mistaken or mysterious (after all, every one of them died before the second coming) had not each account been immediately followed by the story of the transfiguration of Jesus, which the Gospels variously date between six and eight days after that confession on the road to Caesarea Philippi (see also Matthew 17:1–8; Mark 9:2–8).

Clearly this incident is seen by the writers as fulfilling Jesus' words. 'Some'—in fact, just three of them, Peter, James and John— 'saw the kingdom of God', saw Jesus in the glory of heaven. It's a strange and mystic scene, a vision in the correct meaning of the word, unique in the Gospel accounts. It made a profound impact on those who experienced it. John's Gospel says, 'We have seen his glory, the glory as of a father's only son' (1:14). The second letter of Peter claims that 'we had been eyewitnesses of his majesty. For he received honour and glory from God the Father when that voice was conveyed to him by the Majestic Glory, saying, "This is my Son, my Beloved, with whom I am well pleased." We ourselves heard this voice come from heaven, while we were with him on the holy mountain' (2 Peter 1:16–18). Even if, as many scholars believe, the letter was not written by Peter himself, he would evidently seem to be the source of this claim. The whole incident, not surprisingly, left a lasting impression on each of the men who was there.

No one would easily forget so dramatic and unexpected an event. Over the previous few days, the disciples' journey of faith seemed to have taken a dramatic new turn. First of all, they were more or less cornered into confessing that Jesus was the Messiah, expressing openly what, we assume, had simply been a growing inner conviction. Then they were faced with the daunting warning that the Messiah Jesus was to go up to Jerusalem and there be put to death. They were also told that they, his disciples, would need to 'take up their cross' and be prepared to lose their lives for his sake—and 'some of them' would see the glory of Christ's kingdom before they died.

Next, the inner core of the group of disciples, Peter, James and John, were led up a mountain (traditionally, Mount Tabor). Jesus moved a little way off to pray. While he was doing so, the Gospels record, his appearance was 'changed'—'transfigured,' says Matthew 17:2: 'his face shone like the sun'. His clothes 'became dazzling white, such as no fuller on earth could bleach them' (Mark 9:3). A fuller was a person employed to bleach clothes, often by treading them in a large vat with his own feet. The comparison seems somewhat banal for so transcendent an event, but at least it shows how the Gospel writers struggled to put into words the testimony of their sources.

Then, even more surprisingly, two figures appeared with Jesus on the mountain, whom the watchers identified as Moses and Elijah. How they thus identified them we are not told, but it does seem to be a fact that we can often identify people in dreams, for instance, even without visual evidence. At any rate, they recognized the deep significance of the two visitors: Moses, the great bearer of God's Law, Elijah the first of the mighty prophets of Israel. Here were the Law and the Prophets meeting on the hillside with the newly confessed Messiah.

The disciples were struck dumb—except for Peter, who was congenitally incapable of dumbness (a weakness with which I wholly sympathize). He felt it necessary to make a fatuous suggestion. The fact that he knew it was fatuous is captured by his faithful reporter, Mark: 'He did not know what to say, for they were terrified' (9:6). Peter's proposal was simple but both impractical and superficial: 'let us make three dwellings, one for you, one for Moses, and one for Elijah' (v. 5). In other words, 'let's capture the moment', as though this powerful but fleeting vision of eternity could be turned into a sacred memorial on the hillside. It's not unknown, of course, for us to wish to trap our moments of spiritual insight or special blessing, instead of committing them into God's precious gift of grateful memory.

Moses and Elijah were, we are told, 'talking' with Jesus, but only Luke offers an explanation of the subject of their conversation: the Messiah's 'departure, which he was about to accomplish at Jerusalem' (9:31). 'Departure' is literally 'exodus', and the fact that he would 'accomplish' it suggests that all three saw it as a fulfilment rather than an unplanned tragedy.

At this moment a cloud overshadowed the mountain—often, in biblical language, a sign of the presence of the glory of God. The fearful disciples then heard a voice: 'This is my Son, my Chosen; listen to him!' (v. 35). These words are quite similar to the ones heard at the baptism of Jesus by John, but with one significant change of message. At the baptism the voice said, 'This is my Son, the Beloved; with you I am well pleased' (Mark 1:11). Now the identification is the same ('My Son, the Chosen') but the message is not for Jesus but for the disciples: 'Listen to him!' The important question here is one of emphasis. Was it '*listen* to him' or was it 'listen to *him*'? I prefer the latter, mainly because it fits in with the story that has preceded it and relates the message to the event. Moses (the Law) and Elijah (the Prophets) have talked with Jesus, and the disciples are now told that in the new dispensation their priority is to listen to him, to Jesus, even (presumably) ahead of Law and Prophets. If that interpretation is correct, then this is a seminal moment in the history of revelation. There is now a new voice of God, a new agent of truth, and he is Jesus, the 'Chosen', the Messiah of God.

The final scene seems to underline that message, because each Gospel writer records it in similar words: 'Jesus was found alone' (Luke); 'They saw no one with them any more, but only Jesus' (Mark); 'They saw no one except Jesus himself alone' (Matthew). 'Only Jesus'! That seems to be the final and most powerful message of this amazing story of the transfiguration.

The disciples had confessed Jesus to be the Messiah a week earlier. Now, through these chosen representatives, they were given the confirmation that what they had spoken in faith was true in fact. Jesus is the Messiah; he is the 'Chosen of God'; he is the voice of the living God and his agent of truth on earth. From now on, whatever other doubts and fears arose, none of them (not even Judas Iscariot, I suspect) would doubt for a moment that they were following in the footsteps of the Messiah.

A reflection

First the confession, then the confirmation: that is the normal pattern of discipleship. After those comes commission, for these same disciples were to become increasingly aware that the faith they had confessed and the confirmation they had experienced were given so that they could be commissioned for lives of witness and service.

Day 5: The first Sunday of Lent

THE UNENCUMBERED FOLLOWER

READ MATTHEW 19:20–22.

Key verse: 'If you wish to be perfect, go, sell your possessions, and give the money to the poor, and you will have treasure in heaven; then come, follow me' (v. 21).

On these Sundays of Lent we shall be reflecting on the theme of 'following', picking up the Lenten discipline of walking in the way of the cross. Every Christian is a follower of Jesus: there is no simpler or more accurate description of what it means to be his disciple. We follow his example, we follow his teaching and we follow his will. In this passage, the encounter of Jesus with the man known as the 'rich young ruler', we are faced with the cost of following the Saviour.

The young man had approached Jesus with a deceptively simple, almost disingenuous question: 'What good deed must I do to have eternal life?' (v. 16). The answer he got was a standard one for a Jew of the time: 'Keep the commandments.' The young man was able to reply—apparently truthfully—that he had kept them all, some ancient manuscripts even adding the words 'from my youth'. He was, in other words, a devout and observant Jew.

Jesus didn't challenge his claim, although he may have felt it was rather a sweeping one to make. Instead, he raised the stakes: 'If you wish to be perfect, go, sell your possessions, and give the money to the poor, and you will have treasure in heaven; then come, follow me.'

It is interesting that in various other conversations Jesus had with people about discipleship, this is the only occasion when he stipulated that giving all one's possessions away was a necessary condition of following him. Not even the wealthy and influential Nicodemus, who came to Jesus by night with a similar question, was told to abandon his possessions (John 3:1–10). This suggests that possessions were particularly important, even essential, elements in this young man's life. Jesus knew that unless he let go of them he would for ever be an encumbered disciple, not really free to follow Jesus, his loyalties split between acquiring and keeping his wealth and following the one who had nowhere even to lay his head (Luke 9:58).

We don't have to be wealthy to be obsessed with possessions. Sometimes, acquiring and keeping the little we have can also dominate our thinking. What is certain is that those who focus on money or possessions will always be, at best, second-class disciples, because to follow an unencumbered leader we too need to be unencumbered. That may not (probably will not) require the kind of gesture asked of this would-be disciple, but it will demand a willingness to be stripped of those handicapping 'weights' that slowed down the runners in an athletics race (see Hebrews 12:1). Lent is probably a good time to re-examine our priorities to see if we, like the rich young ruler, are handicapping ourselves in the marathon run to eternal life.

A reflection

'Let us also lay aside every weight and the sin that clings so closely, and let us run with perseverance the race that is set before us, looking to Jesus the pioneer and perfecter of our faith' (Hebrews 12:1–2).

Day 6: Monday

FOLLOWING IN THE
REAL WORLD

READ LUKE 9:37–43.

Key verse: 'You faithless and perverse generation, how much longer must I be with you and bear with you? Bring your son here' (v. 41).

Londoners used to say, 'After the Lord Mayor's Show comes the dustcart.' It's equally true that after the mountain-top experience comes the valley of despair. No one can live life exclusively among the stars, just as we feel that it is wrong and unfair that some people seem condemned to stay in the dust. The Gospel writers faithfully record the order of events: transfiguration and glory up the mountain; sorrow, despair and failure at the foot of it. The three disciples who had just seen the Lord in his heavenly splendour then watched as the same Lord faced the failure of the other nine disciples to meet a wretched case of human need. It was Moses and Elijah up the mountain, and a desperate father and his tormented son at the foot of it.

The sight drew from Jesus the words of our key verse—strange words, in a way, because they seem to focus on the frustration he felt rather than the cruel situation he faced. They may, as many commentators suggest, be directed at the disciples, to whom a few days earlier he had specifically given 'authority over all demons and to cure diseases' (v. 1) but who had now dismally failed to help the father and his son. The words might equally, however, be directed at a society—indeed, a fallen world—in which people created in the image of God could end up as wretched and forlorn as the young boy in front of him. After all, he addressed the words to 'a faithless and perverse generation', as though the cause of his frustration was something wider and more all-embracing than the failures of the embryonic band of apostles.

The Gospels frequently record that, faced with human sickness and suffering, Jesus was 'moved with compassion', but no English words can quite convey the depth of feeling that the phrase expresses in Greek. 'Gut-wrenching' is probably as near as we can get to it: the sight 'turned his stomach over'. In some cases (for example, the healing of the first leper to confront Jesus after his baptism: Mark 1:41), there is ancient manuscript support for the word 'anger' instead of 'compassion'. In other words, to the Son of God on earth the outworking of the consequences of millennia of human disobedience seen in suffering, injustice and disease were not simply sad but offensive. This was not what the Creator had intended or willed, but a corruption or distortion of the beauty of his creation. At the sight of it his Son was appalled, deeply moved, even angry.

So the sad figures now before him—the grieving father, the boy caught in an endless sequence of fits of an epileptic kind—were the living, weeping evidences of the need for the incarnation, for a new kind of inner healing. 'Bring him to *me*,' Jesus said (Mark 9:19), echoing perhaps the divine message on the mountain, 'Listen to *him*'. Only the Son of man who is also Son of God could reverse the consequences of the fall. Only the redeeming power of God could transform sickness into wholeness.

Jesus dealt with the boy's condition by 'casting out' the cause of it. This is described as a 'spirit of uncleanness' (literally), which makes the NRSV's use of the word 'demon' (Luke 9:42) potentially misleading. The boy's illness, which modern medicine would prob-ably diagnose as epilepsy, was caused by something in his physical or mental situation, and it could only be healed (he could only be 'made whole') when that something had been removed.

In Luke's account—in contrast with Mark's, for instance—the removal was devastatingly uncomplicated. Jesus 'rebuked the unclean spirit, healed the boy, and gave him back to his father' (v. 42). No wonder 'all were astounded at the greatness of God' (v. 43). The 'all' undoubtedly included the nine disciples who had so signally failed to help him and who, shortly afterwards, would be complaining that other 'unauthorized' disciples were successfully doing what they had failed to do, 'casting out demons' in the name of Jesus (v. 49).

Before that, however, Jesus had repeated his sobering warning to them. Despite the glory of the mountain and the power of the healing down below, nothing had changed in the divine plan. They were still to go to Jerusalem; the Son of Man would still be betrayed into human hands (v. 44). The disciples, despite their recent confession of Jesus as Messiah, 'did not understand this saying; its meaning was concealed from them, so that they could not perceive it' (v. 45). Eventually they would understand, but for now the whole concept of a suffering Messiah giving his life for his people was literally beyond their comprehension. At the proper time, all would be revealed and the glorious potential of sacrifice as a way of salvation would be their constant theme.

A reflection

Following a time of spiritual blessing or refreshment, when we feel at peace with ourselves and God, there often comes a time of spiritual challenge. It happened to Elijah, after his magnificent triumph over the priests of Baal on Mount Carmel (1 Kings 18:46; 19:4). The mountain top is not far from the plain of despair. The answer (which we find difficult to comprehend at times) is that the same Lord is with us on both.

Day 7: Tuesday

ALL ARE WELCOME

READ LUKE 9:46–50.

Key verse: 'The least among all of you is the greatest' (v. 48).

We have been told that the disciples did not understand, at this point, the meaning of Jesus' words about suffering and death. So unperceptive were they that they launched straight into an argument among themselves over which one of them was the 'greatest'. Presumably they still held on to the notion that Jesus, as Messiah, was about to restore the kingdom to Israel and appoint them, his chosen followers, as leading lights in the new regime. The notion of hierarchy, or what we might more crudely call 'pecking order', is so deeply rooted in human thinking that most of us can readily see why this topic was so important to them. If Jesus was the Messiah, and the kingdom was about to be restored, then the new 'David' seated on the royal throne in Jerusalem would need some trusted courtiers and officials. Surely the Twelve, already chosen as his associates and companions, should be at the front of the queue for such positions? Time, then, to discuss who would qualify for which office and in what order.

It all seemed eminently logical, but they were wrong in profound and fundamental ways. In fact, Jesus pointed out, using a young child as a visual aid, 'the least among all of you'—the weak and vulnerable—is the 'greatest'. Jesus himself could be welcomed by welcoming this child—a nobody in the world's eyes but in God's sight precious.

We are accustomed to speaking of children like this one as vulnerable and dependent, but in first-century Israel it went further than that. Children were plentiful because a large family was, in effect, the parents' pension. Boys were especially valued for that reason, but girls could bring in dowries and so help the family economy too. That may sound callous and casual, but the sentimentalization of childhood is a relatively recent phenomenon, and we shall fail to see the real thrust of this little scene if we think of it solely as the contrast of a powerless child with an ambitious disciple. It is more stark than that. The child, in social and status terms, was a nobody, yet the child was in truth the 'greatest', because he or she was made in the image of God and could be welcomed in the name of Jesus. Like Jesus, the child claimed no social status but was valued and cherished by the heavenly Father, even if despised and rejected by the world. This child, in other words, was greater than any of those who sought status and power without recognizing its source.

The disciples, undaunted by the rebuke, then raised another issue of status. 'We saw someone casting out demons in your name, and we tried to stop him, because he does not follow with us' (v. 49) Oh dear! As we saw yesterday, this anonymous 'someone' was doing (apparently effectively) what they had been authorized by Jesus to do but had failed to accomplish. But he was 'not one of us': in some religious quarters, that always seems to be the most serious of all sins. For the disciples, of course, this 'someone' was both a rebuke (why couldn't they do it?) and a challenge to their status. He wasn't one of the Twelve, so, in their thinking, he wasn't anywhere in the line for a place of honour in the messianic kingdom.

Yet again Jesus had to rebuke them, though more gently this time. 'Don't stop the irregular healer,' he told them. 'Whoever is not against you is for you' (v. 50). They were to recognize spiritual allies even in the unlikeliest places. More than that, they would need to abandon thoughts of precedence and power if they were to be true representatives of this Messiah. That would be true 'kingdom' thinking, but the disciples hadn't got there yet.

A reflection

In the kingdom of heaven there are no nobodies, because all are valued by God. There is also no hierarchy of somebodies. Every knee bows at the name of Jesus.

Day 8: Wednesday

TRAVELLING LIGHT

READ LUKE 9:1–6.

Key verse: 'Take nothing for your journey, no staff, nor bag, nor bread, nor money—not even an extra tunic (v. 3).

It's just as well that this command of Jesus was directed to his first-century disciples and not the 21st-century holidaymaker. No spare tunic? Watch us as we stagger towards the check-in desk at the airport, dragging behind us huge bags and cases stuffed with an entire wardrobe, plus every conceivable piece of personal equipment we might need to survive a week or a fortnight in a foreign clime. We have forgotten what travelling light really means, which is simply 'roughing it'. Incidentally (and perhaps inexplicably), Mark alone (6:8) permits the dogged disciple to take a staff—but nothing else!

The Christian pilgrim is meant to travel light, unencumbered by the kinds of things that make progress slow and may discourage us from continuing the journey. We have already seen how the weight of riches was judged by Jesus as too heavy for a young man to carry if he wanted to follow him. Now we have the Twelve, or perhaps a wider group of disciples, given their marching orders. Don't encumber yourself with unnecessary baggage. The journey itself is too important for such distractions.

The first-century traveller already travelled light by our standards. He needed to: after all, whatever he took he carried. Only the relatively wealthy would have had a beast of burden. Most people simply walked and carried a load on their backs. It's that load—a familiar sight—that concerns Jesus. Here, the burden is seen by him as a possible spiritual handicap, and we too may have physical burdens that tax and strain our faith—illness, home circumstances, a demanding caring role or work that we find unrewarding or tedious.

There are other burdens, of course, among them financial anxiety or broken relationships. For some people, long working hours or the demands of small children weigh heavily as they try to follow Christ. In one sense, the command to the disciples, while demanding, was at least practicable. They could do it, even if it caused some inconvenience. The requirement to take no prepared meals with them had one positive element to it: it cast them on to the hospitality of the people they visited. They did not come as well-heeled messengers of a 'prosperity gospel' but as simple, penniless, hungry pilgrims looking for somewhere to sleep and something to eat. Perhaps their message of the kingdom was all the more telling for that.

Christian pilgrims who travel light, however, are not left to fend for themselves. In the first place, Jesus also travelled light. At the most obvious level, he also walked, sleeping in the open and depending on others for food and other necessities (Luke 9:58; Mark 15:41). At a more profound level, he offers to share the burden, like an ox yoked to its partner in the field. 'Come to me', he says, 'all you that are weary and are carrying heavy burdens, and I will give you rest. Take my yoke upon you, and learn from me; for I am gentle and humble in heart, and you will find rest for your souls. For my yoke is easy and my burden is light' (Matthew 11:28–30).

In the context of this passage, and at this stage in the ministry of Jesus and the training of the Twelve, we may take these words as applying to their immediate task of proclaiming the good news of the kingdom of God to the 'lost sheep of the house of Israel' (Matthew 10:6). Until that ministry was fulfilled and the people of the covenant had been given every opportunity to respond to the message, the first part of the mission of Jesus was incomplete. The Twelve, and also perhaps the Seventy (Luke 10:1), were to act as an extension of his own ministry, not only proclaiming the kingdom message but also with authority to cast out demons and to heal (9:1–2).

It's not clear from the Gospels exactly how this mission of the disciples fared. Some claimed that they were indeed able to heal and exorcise (10:17), yet nine of the Twelve failed to help the epileptic boy and his distraught father (9:40). Perhaps they were to learn more themselves from this exercise than the people they went to teach. In any case, from the time of the transfiguration we read less and less of a mission by the disciples and more and more of Jesus' mission to the disciples, as he sought to prepare them for the traumatic events that lay ahead in Jerusalem.

The message about travelling light does seem, however, to have struck home and become a permanent element in the lifestyle of the first disciples. The apostle Paul was able to say that he knew what it was to have little and also to have plenty, yet in both conditions he had learned to be content (see Philippians 4:12). Travelling light can help today's disciple, too, to discover the same secret.

A reflection

Travelling light was a practical necessity in the ancient world, where everything you took with you had to be carried. In today's world it is a matter of deliberate choice. To travel light through life is to shed encumbrances—all those trappings that fill our time, empty our bank balance and distort our priorities. To travel light is also a witness to a world in which many have little choice but to do so. Our travelling light may help them to travel at all: we live simply so that they may simply live.

STUMBLING BLOCKS

READ MATTHEW 18:8–9.

Key verse: 'If your hand or your foot causes you to stumble, cut it off and throw it away; it is better for you to enter life maimed or lame than to have two hands or two feet and to be thrown into the eternal fire' (v. 8).

For two years, as they wandered the highways and byways of Galilee, Jesus had been preparing his little band of followers for the moment when they would have to set their faces towards Jerusalem. At first, through mighty acts and words of power, he led them to the awesome realization that their leader and friend was truly the Son of God, the Messiah sent by the Father. Then, on the mount of transfiguration, he confirmed to the inner core of the group that what they had come to believe and had so recently confessed was nothing less than the truth of the matter.

One way and another, as these astonishing facts began to sink in, they tried to make sense of them. For some in the group, they seemed to offer a prospect of power and status, as we have seen. Others may well have been anxious at the implications for the safety of their leader and their own safety. As Jesus spelt out in words of surprising candour the kind of scenario that lay ahead, some may have even begun to wonder whether the price was worth paying. Arrest, suffering and death were promised at the end of the road and, so far as they could see, the only expected gain would be the utterly inexplicable promise that the Son of

Man would be raised from death on the third day.

Then, of course, there was the 'kingdom of heaven', whatever that might be. The disciples had been told that those who made sacrifices for that kingdom's sake would, in due time, be rewarded. Indeed, the Twelve would 'sit on twelve thrones, judging the twelve tribes of Israel' (Matthew 19:28)—but even that apparently cast-iron promise was followed by the warning that 'many who are first will be last, and the last will be first' (v. 30).

The daunting words spoken by Jesus and recorded by the Gospels in today's reading seem to have been intended to spell out the crucial issue of priority—one of the great themes of the teaching of Jesus. 'For what will it profit them,' he would ask his followers, 'if they gain the whole world but forfeit their life?' (Matthew 16:26). For him, the greatest folly of all was to get priorities wrong—to store up goods on earth but ignore treasure in heaven (6:21), to set aside a tithe of mint from the roadside but swindle widows out of their property (23:23), to build a business empire but forget that one day we must answer for our deeds (Luke 12:16–21).

In this passage Jesus uses a literary device that he frequently employs—hyperbole. This involves deliberate exaggeration in order to make a point. We use it if we say, 'I'm dying for a cup of tea' when all we mean is that we're a bit thirsty. Jesus employed it with devastating effect in his teaching to the crowds—describing the Pharisees straining out a gnat and swallowing a camel (Matthew 23:24), for instance, or saying that it would be easier for a camel to get through the eye of a needle than for a rich man to get into the kingdom of heaven (Mark 10:25). Here, he is certainly not advocating self-mutilation, but presenting his listeners with a stark set of priorities in vivid and memorable terms. 'If it came to it...' he is saying, in effect, it would be preferable to go into eternal life without a hand or a foot than to go into the eternal fire in one piece. Put like that, it sounds eminently reasonable!

Jesus did not want his disciples to be under any illusions. The choice they had made to follow him wherever he went would inevitably involve them in some strange, painful and costly experiences. What they had to be clear about was that, in the end, they had chosen the road to life and, however rocky and difficult it proved to be, it was the right road to be on.

With this challenge ringing in their ears, it seems that the long process of preparation for the decisive journey to Jerusalem was complete. Now, at last, they would be ready for what lay ahead, their priorities clear, their final goal established. That, at least, was the master plan, but human weakness, circumstances, events and (sadly) sin would put it under intense pressure over the days that lay ahead.

A reflection

Jesus never promised his disciples (and doesn't promise them now) an easy road to follow. After all, as he had said, there is an easy road for those who choose it, but it leads to 'destruction'. There is also, on the other hand, a road that is narrow and hard, but it leads to life (Matthew 7:13–14). They had made the choice between the roads to follow, and so must we.

Part Two

SETTING OUT FOR JERUSALEM

Day 10: Friday

FOLLOW THE LEADER

READ LUKE 9:51, 57–62.

Key verse: When the days drew near for him to be taken up, he set his face to go to Jerusalem (v. 51).

At last the final journey to Jerusalem begins. The Gospel writers offer a picture of dramatic contrasts: Jesus 'setting his face' to go to his destiny, the disciples following with understandable reluctance. Mark puts it in visual terms. 'Jesus was walking ahead of them; they were amazed, and those who followed were afraid' (10:32). The picture is of the Master striding purposefully ahead—even though he knew more certainly than anyone else that the destiny he seemed so eager to grasp was his death—while behind him came the Twelve, amazed (presumably at his eagerness), and a larger group of disciples who were simply afraid.

Luke speaks of it all in terms of a date with destiny: 'When the days drew near for [Jesus] to be taken up…'. The phrase 'taken up' is an intriguing one. At its simplest and most literal level, it could mean simply that he was going 'up' to Jerusalem, the holy city, but the phrase has an ancient resonance. Elijah was 'taken up' into heaven (2 Kings 1:11)—and wasn't it Elijah with whom Jesus had recently been conversing on the mount of the transfiguration? John 12:32 speaks of Jesus being glorified by being 'lifted up' on the cross. There might also be a hint here of Moses (the other figure on the mountain), who was never seen after his death on Mount Nebo and whose tomb was at an unknown location.

In any case, the whole picture is of a moment of decision. The Galilee mission is over. There will be few miracles now until the greatest of them all, the resurrection, and Jesus will not say much to the crowds who were such a feature of the first part of the Gospels. From now on, the theme is discipleship—what it means to follow Jesus—and the ones under instruction are the Twelve, and the fearful disciples behind them. We feel that there is not much time left. Suddenly an urgency enters the story. A threatening and powerful opponent awaits them in Jerusalem but, even before then, the very first people they encounter on their journey, the Samaritans, whose villages straddled the road south, refuse to have anything to do with them because they are heading towards the hated seat of the temple powers.

The biggest problems, however, seem to be in the ranks of the disciples themselves. The change of tone—the switch from the familiar, quiet lanes and villages of Galilee, with their largely welcoming crowds, to the road to Jerusalem, the seat of the religious opposition—apparently took them by surprise. Now the message of Jesus also seems to have taken on a harder edge. The emphasis is on the cost of discipleship. The casual 'let's-jump-on-the-bandwagon' kind of follower is no longer welcome. 'If you want to come with me,' Jesus says, in effect, 'this is what it means. Be absolutely sure you understand this, because from now on we cannot carry passengers in the team.'

The dialogue in Luke 9 between three would-be disciples and Jesus makes the point powerfully. Each expresses a willingness to be a follower of Jesus. The first adds no conditions, but nevertheless gets only a warning in response: 'Foxes have holes, and birds of the air have nests, but the Son of Man has nowhere to lay his head' (v. 58). Those seeking comfort, status or the dignities of power had better look elsewhere.

The second applicant does add a condition to his response to the call of Jesus. It seems perfectly reasonable: 'Let me first bury my father' (v. 59). The problem is that we don't know if his father was yet dead. His answer could mean, 'I'll follow you after my father has died—when the family business and inheritance have been sorted out.' The Lord's response is brief and dismissive: 'Let the dead bury their own dead' (v. 60). For the disciple, there is a greater priority: the proclamation of the kingdom of God. We may be sure that Jesus, who wept at the tomb of his friend Lazarus, was not being indifferent to the pain of bereavement or lacking proper respect for those who have died. As so often, the issue is one of priorities. As William Barclay puts it in his commentary on Luke (St Andrews Press, 1983), 'The point Jesus was making was that in everything there is a crucial moment; if that moment is missed, the thing will most likely never be done at all' (p. 132).

That issue is even sharper for the last would-be disciple. He would follow Jesus but... 'let me first say farewell to those at my home' (v. 61). What was involved in such 'farewells' was a great deal more complicated than simply a hug and kiss all round. An eastern farewell might have taken several days and might also have involved gathering the wider family circle. In all probability, this was a request for a period of delay: 'Lord, I will follow you, but not yet.' Jesus detected the signs of someone who would be for ever looking back at what he had left behind rather than pressing on towards the final goal.

In any case (and this is surely the central message of this exchange), those who set out to carry the kingdom message must have their priorities clear. It might involve homelessness. It might mean the severing of sacred family ties. It certainly demanded that the disciple should have eyes only on the goal ahead and not be constantly looking back over his shoulder at what might have been: 'No one who puts his hand to the plough and looks back is fit for the kingdom of God' (v. 62).

A reflection

Jesus does not ask his followers to do anything that he was not willing to do himself. He emptied himself of all glory and status when he was born at Bethlehem, and set his sights solely on doing 'the will of him who sent me' (John 5:30).

Day 11: Saturday

TO LEAD IS TO SERVE

READ MARK 10:41–45.

Key verse: 'Whoever wishes to become great among you must be your servant, and whoever wishes to be first among you must be slave of all' (vv. 43–44).

The sons of Zebedee, James and John, the fishermen recruited by Jesus from the shores of Lake Galilee at the start of his ministry, came to him with what seems on the surface an impertinent and self-seeking request. They began by asking Jesus to 'do for us whatever we ask of you' (v. 35), possibly prompted by the memory of some advice Jesus had given the disciples earlier: 'Ask, and it will be given to you' (Matthew 7:7). That may be the kindest explanation of what otherwise looks like an attempt to get one move ahead of the other disciples and reserve for themselves the chief places of honour in the coming kingdom of God. Their request was that one of them would sit at the right hand of Jesus in his glory, and the other on his left (Mark 10:37).

As so often, Jesus answered a question (in true Jewish style) with another one: 'Are you able to drink the cup that I drink, or be baptized with the baptism that I am baptized with?' (v. 38). The 'cup' was undoubtedly the cup of divine judgment and the 'baptism' was his death on the cross (see Jeremiah 25:15; Luke 12:50). Rather impetuously, James and John replied that they could, and (perhaps to their surprise) Jesus agreed with them: they would indeed suffer for the kingdom, and one of them, at least, would die for it. However, the seats at his side in his glory were not his to allocate. They were for those 'for whom it has been prepared' (v. 40), presumably by the Father.

That was the end of the conversation, but when the other ten disciples heard of this little encounter they were furious with James and John. Why should the brothers assume superiority in rank over the others? If there were to be honours, shouldn't they be shared out? It was the old pecking order dispute all over again.

Once again Jesus had to call them to order, and the words of today's passage are the heart of what he told them. They had not yet understood the central kingdom principle. They had not even begun to understand what messiahship meant to Jesus, but were thinking purely in human or worldly terms. So he repeated what he had already told them and had illustrated by setting a small child before them: the kingdom of God does not come through power or rank or status but through service. This principle applied even to Jesus himself: 'the Son of Man came not to be served but to serve, and to give his life a ransom for many' (v. 45). He was a Messiah who would serve and suffer for his people, paying the price for their release from the consequences of their sins.

Some years ago, I preached at a passing-out service at the Royal Military Academy, Sandhurst, where officers are trained for many of the world's finest armies. The chaplain had told me in advance that the Academy's motto was 'To lead is to serve'. I could have asked for no better text for my sermon, relating it to this very passage in Mark's Gospel. Those who wish to be great must learn to be servants of the others; those who wish to be the most important in the group must be 'slaves of all' (v. 44). It was a lesson that Jesus vividly illustrated in the upper room, when he, not the Gentile slave they were expecting, washed the disciples' feet (John 13:1–14). On that occasion, he explained precisely the same message, that they also should serve one another rather than argue about precedence. It was, and is, a hard lesson to learn, and it's sad that throughout the history of the Church much of its internal conflict has been about roles, status and office rather than the overriding principle of service.

A reflection

Jesus Christ is the 'servant king', and the disciples are not above their Master!

Day 12: Sunday

TO SERVE IS TO FOLLOW

READ JOHN 12:25–26.

Key verse: 'Whoever serves me must follow me, and where I am, there will my servant be also. Whoever serves me, the Father will honour' (v. 26).

Today's passage, while certainly on our Sunday theme of 'following', also reinforces the message of establishing priorities, which is such a prominent emphasis in Jesus' teaching as he and the disciples set out on their final journey together. He sets their destinies alongside his own. He is the 'grain of wheat' (v. 24) that must fall to the earth and die before it can produce a harvest. Just as he was prepared to lose his life for them, so they must also value their earthly lives lightly, so that eternal life will be theirs.

All of this follows a consistent pattern of discipleship. To serve Jesus is to follow him. Revelation describes the saints in heaven as those who 'follow the Lamb wherever he goes' (14:4). It has to be said that those who live by this principle will inevitably find themselves in some demanding and challenging situations. Following the Lamb has taken some people to far-flung places, put many lives in jeopardy, led martyrs into the arenas of the Roman world to face wild beasts and gladiators and drawn others to slums and hovels and refugee camps. Following Jesus has never been a boring or predictable calling, but his disciples are not asked to go where he has not already been.

There is a further truth in this passage, and it is a clear promise:

'Where I am, there will my servant be' (12:26). Not only that, but 'whoever serves me, the Father will honour'. At the very end of his earthly ministry, as he gave the great commission to the apostles to 'make disciples of all nations', Jesus promised that he would be with them always, 'to the end of the age' (Matthew 28:19–20). In return for the disciples' commitment, he would be with them, and they would be with him. The promises are similar, but not identical. The first gives the assurance that Jesus would be with them in their struggles and their challenges; he would provide strength for the tasks and the wisdom of the Holy Spirit to guide them. The other promise looks to the future. Wherever he is, they will be. As he told them on the fateful night of his betrayal, he was leaving them, but only so that he could 'come again' and take them to himself, 'so that where I am, there you may be also' (John 14:3). This is the 'honour' that the Father has for them—not seats of power in the heavenly kingdom but the eternal presence of Jesus himself in the Father's glory. They would follow him wherever he led them, but the place to which he was eventually leading them was the endless fulfilment of the kingdom of heaven—what John's Gospel simply calls 'eternal life'.

A reflection

O Jesus, thou hast promised
To all who follow thee,
That where thou art in glory
There shall thy servant be;
And, Jesus, I have promised
To serve thee to the end:
O give me grace to follow,
My Master and my friend.
JOHN ERNEST BODE (1816–74)

Day 13: Monday

CURED, OR HEALED?

READ LUKE 17:11–19.

Key verse: Then he said to him, 'Get up and go on your way; your faith has made you well' (v. 19).

Possibly because of the hostility of the Samaritan villagers, who resented the presence of 13 Jewish men on their way to Jerusalem, with its despised temple, Jesus and the disciples took the slightly less direct route from the north along the border between Samaria and Galilee. As they approached a village, they met a group of ten 'lepers'. No one is quite sure what 'leprosy' meant in biblical times —probably not the disease we know by that name today. It may have been a contagious skin condition, which largely incapacitated its victims and certainly cut them off from normal human contacts. Consequently, many 'lepers' lived in small colonies, perhaps based in caves or tents, obeying the injunctions set out in Leviticus 13 and 14, and avoiding the sort of contact with other people that might have caused resentment or anger.

When the group of lepers saw Jesus and his companions, they consequently kept their distance, but called out to him, 'Jesus, Master, have mercy on us!' (v. 13). Clearly, even people in leper colonies had heard of him and his reputation as a healer and, by some means or other, they were able to recognize him. Jesus' response was immediate: they should go and show themselves to the priests (to obtain a certificate that they were clear of the disease)—a formula precisely laid down in the Mosaic law. The very act of going would be an exercise of considerable faith, because presumably the priests would not take kindly to being faced with ten diseased men all demanding certificates.

In fact, as they went, they were all 'made clean' (v. 14). Seeing this, nine of them hurried off towards the priests, while one—but only one—turned back to shout praises to God for his healing. He also threw himself down at the feet of Jesus and thanked him.

'And he was a Samaritan' (v. 16). Just as it was a Samaritan who acted as a true neighbour to the man who fell among thieves (Luke 10:33), so now a Samaritan is the only one to return and give praise to God—not an observant Jew but, as Jesus described him, 'this foreigner' (17:18). It was, in context, a rebuke to the sense of spiritual superiority that had infiltrated the people of the covenant. In a timeless sense, it represents a rebuke to all of us who think that absolute doctrinal rectitude and precise ritual observance are more important than a simple faith and a grateful heart.

There is, however, another element in this story that deserves attention. The nine lepers are described as being 'made clean'. The grateful Samaritan, by contrast, was 'made well'. This is a distinction—reflected in the use of different verbs—that is made from time to time by all the Gospel writers and therefore, presumably, reflects an understanding that the disciples had gained from Jesus himself. Some people, it seems, were 'cured' at his hands, but others were 'made well'—or, more correctly, 'made whole'. It does not go beyond the textual evidence to assert that the nine lepers had their bodies cured of a horrible disease but that the Samaritan was also made whole in body, mind and spirit. The word translated 'made well' carries strong implications. It is used in the New Testament of the way of salvation (1 Corinthians 15:2), of being healed or restored to health (Matthew 9:21), and even of being saved or preserved from being lost (Matthew 16:25). Without wishing to labour the point, the distinction between being 'made clean', or cured of leprosy, and being made whole as a human being is significant, to say the least, and it was the spontaneous act of praise and gratitude on the part of the

Samaritan which distinguished his experience from that of the others.

Again, the Samaritan was told by Jesus to 'go on your way' (Luke 17:19). At the simple level, that would mean he could resume normal life, travelling where he wished and meeting people without restriction or barrier. Yet, as we shall see again in the story of Bartimaeus, the use of the word 'way' would have been picked up by the first Christians as almost a coded formula. After all, they were called, and dubbed themselves, the 'people of the Way' (see Acts 24:14). Could it be, then, that this grateful Samaritan himself became a follower of Jesus?

A reflection

In our Western society, where health is a media obsession and our cupboards overflow with bottles of pills, it's probably worth considering from time to time what 'health' really means—in English as well as Aramaic or Greek. 'Health' is wholeness, and salvation is nothing less than being made completely whole as a human being, in body, mind and spirit. That wholeness will only be complete, of course, when we are 'changed' (in body, mind and spirit) as we move from mortal life to the eternal one, at the final resurrection (see 1 Corinthians 15:50–57).

Day 14: Tuesday

THE INNER KINGDOM

READ LUKE 17:20–21.

Key verse: 'In fact, the kingdom of God is among you' (v. 21)

The Pharisees were a Jewish sect active from the time of the Hasmoneans (about the middle of the second century BC), through the period covered by the Gospels and until the destruction of the temple and the dispersion of the Jews in AD70. On the whole, they get a bad press in the Gospels, especially Matthew's, probably reflecting the controversies between Jews and Christians that came about during and after the apostolic period. Luke, however, seems to have recognized that, in some ways, the Pharisees were rather closer to the teaching and practice of Jesus than were the scribes (teachers of the law) or the temple hierarchy.

The Pharisees were a reformist group, more concerned with how people kept the law than with the detail of the law itself. They believed that only a reformed and renewed Judaism could possibly lead to the liberation of the people from the yoke of occupation and the sacrilege that often went with it. They had strong links with the governing classes but were not themselves a governing class. They did see themselves as guardians of a sacred tradition and were sensitive about the impact of anyone, like Jesus, who seemed to threaten the stability of Jewish society. On the resurrection of the dead they took the same theological position as Jesus, against the equally influential Sadducees, but were prepared to make pragmatic alliances with the Sadducees and with the Herodians (supporters of the Herod family, who collaborated with the Romans) if they felt it would help to maintain stability and curtail the power of the Roman administration.

Their name has become synonymous, in our everyday language, with a nit-picking observance of rules and regulations, but that is probably too simple a description of their beliefs. There were clearly 'good' Pharisees: indeed, Luke refers to two occasions when Jesus was invited to dinner by Pharisees (11:37; 14:1). What Jesus seems to have found deeply objectionable was the hypocrisy of some Pharisees (and scribes) who were busy telling everyone else how to do what God required while ignoring it themselves. No religious movement, however, has ever had a monopoly on hypocrisy.

From time to time, Pharisees had ventured up into Galilee to cast a critical eye on this new teacher and prophet, Jesus. There, alongside the scribes, they formed the opinion that he was taking to himself altogether too much authority. Issues of authority always worry those who see themselves as the guardians of truth. Now, as Jesus and his disciples slowly made their way south, the Pharisees had less distance to go to carry out their examination.

On this occasion they had a perfectly reasonable question to put: 'When is the kingdom of God coming?' (v. 20). After all, Jesus constantly preached about the kingdom. Indeed, 'the kingdom of God' was his message. The Pharisees too believed that one day the reign of God would come on earth and the kingdom be restored to Israel. What intrigued them, and many Jews at the time, was *when?* For 300 years they had been under enemy (pagan) occupation. Had God forgotten his people? As the 'kingdom' was clearly very important to Jesus, it was natural that they should seek his opinion on the subject. In fact, their question was put as though seeking not his opinion but his judgment on the issue, almost as if they were conceding to him the authority to decide on such a profound question.

A reasonable question deserved, and got, a reasonable answer, even though it might not have been the one they expected or wanted to hear. What Jesus did in his answer was to highlight the deep difference between his understanding of the kingdom of God and the popular understanding at the time: 'The kingdom of God is not coming with things that can be observed; nor will they say, "Look, here it is!" or "There it is!"' (vv. 20–21). The kingdom of God, in other words, is not something physical and visible, like an army on the march or a king on a throne or a fortified city. People wouldn't watch the kingdom of God arrive like a military takeover or a spiritual coup d'état that replaces a corrupt government with a more just and godly one. In one sense, there wouldn't be anything to see. The kingdom of God is perceived with the inner eye, with the insight of the Spirit of God, because it is about a totally new way of living. In fact, Jesus said, 'the kingdom of God is among you' (v. 21).

A great deal hinges on that word 'among', so the fact that it is sometimes translated 'in' or 'within' makes it slightly confusing. The little Greek preposition (such a tiny word to bear such a weight of truth) is the root of our word 'interior' and can mean 'among', but equally often means 'inside' or 'within'. In these circumstances, it is only by looking at the context and the general flow of the argument that we can tease out the likely meaning. On those grounds, 'in', 'within' or 'inside' seem to me better translations than 'among', although we mustn't lose sight of the fact that the 'you' is plural and it is evidently true that the kingdom of God is a collective rather than an individual phenomenon. As 'I' enter the kingdom through an act of repentance and faith, I am immediately a member of a new society, which lives to new, divinely set standards with fresh goals and ambitions and with a revolutionary purpose. The kingdom of God exists to live out on earth the life of heaven—its peace, justice, righteousness and love.

We can't see that with the naked eye! The beauty and truth of the kingdom of God are experienced rather than observed. The Pharisees wanted a date for its arrival, but it was 'among' them now, in lives that had repented and believed, in wills that had been retuned to God's standards. In that sense, the kingdom certainly was among them but, because of its interior nature, they couldn't see it unless or until they too entered through the narrow gate and found it for themselves.

Years ago, as a new Christian, I remember listening to a talk by an elderly bishop who spoke about the 'inwardness of true religion'. What he said then, every bit of 50 years ago, I can remember now, because it came to me as a startling new insight. Religion isn't about outward signs and rituals and observances—or rather, if it is, it is only the visible part of the invisible essence. True religion is a matter of heart, mind and will, even though that inwardness will be reflected in visible patterns of behaviour and decision-making.

'The kingdom of God is within, or inside, or among you.' It wasn't to be found in the great temple; not in programmes of religious reformation or obligatory acts of self-denial; not in outward observances, no matter how seriously and sincerely performed. They might or might not be signs of the kingdom, but the kingdom itself would come when the rebellious will of human beings finally submitted to the just and gracious will of their Creator, and not before.

A reflection

We pray, 'Your kingdom come' and immediately add, 'Your will be done on earth as it is in heaven.' There is the heart of the kingdom—obedience to the will of the one who made us and knows what is best for us. The kingdom of God exists wherever people live by and model its principle of justice, love and peace.

Day 15: Wednesday

TRYING TO SEE JESUS

READ LUKE 19:1–10.

Key verse: [Zacchaeus] ran ahead and climbed a sycomore tree to see him, because he was going to pass that way (v. 4).

Jesus and the disciples were now approaching Jericho, one of the world's oldest inhabited towns. It lies to the east of Jerusalem, about six miles north of the Dead Sea and 900 feet below sea level. It stood for centuries on the main trade route to the north and, because of its springs of water, it earned the title 'City of Palms'. I remember driving down from Jerusalem along the road through the wilderness of Judea and being struck by the vision of trees and bushes that seemed suddenly to appear below me. Orange trees line the town's dusty roads and there is fresh fruit for sale everywhere.

Jesus and his disciples had made their way along the valley of the Jordan (thus avoiding Samaria). Jericho would be the last place of importance that they would pass through on their journey up to Jerusalem. The Gospels record two incidents during their brief stay there and both involve eyesight. The appealing story of a tax collector, Zacchaeus, is the first of them.

The 'tax collectors'—rather unhelpfully called 'publicans' in the King James Bible—were very unpopular members of Jewish society at the time. The Romans had invented a simple method of extracting taxes from reluctant conquered peoples: they used local talent. By employing those who knew the district, its businesses, the identity of the richest people and even the methods employed locally to avoid payment, the Romans were able to collect the money due without needing to make much direct contact with resentful contributors. The collectors were not paid a wage as such, but were allowed to add a percentage to the sum due, which they kept as payment for work done.

From the Romans' point of view, the system worked well enough. One armed soldier standing by each tax collection booth was generally enough to ensure that there was no trouble and the taxes were collected regularly and efficiently.

From the point of view of the residents, however, there were two enormous drawbacks. The first was related to that 'percentage' which the collectors could add for themselves. The authorities do not seem to have been very bothered how large it was or even how much it varied from person to person, so long as the actual tax revenue was collected. As a result, the tax collectors charged whatever they thought they could get away with, which—given the presence of armed Roman soldiers—was usually a great deal over and above the official tax.

The second drawback was implicit in the nature of the tax collectors' role. They were serving the enemy, doing the dirty work for the occupying power. In World War II, there was a Norwegian political leader who ruled the country on behalf of the occupying Nazi power and used his position to carry out their policies of suppression. His name was Vidkun Quisling, and today the *Oxford English Dictionary* defines a quisling as 'a traitor collaborating with an occupying enemy force'. At a rather less exalted level, the tax collectors of the first century were quislings and for that, as much as their extortionate demands, they were universally hated and despised by the native population.

Such a one was Zacchaeus, a Jewish collaborator with the Romans, who presumably plied his unpopular trade in Jericho. He was, Luke 19 tells us, a 'chief tax collector' (v. 2) and rich. He was also (though this was no fault of his own) short of stature. When he heard that Jesus was passing through Jericho, he determined to try to see him, but the size of the crowds and his own limited stature meant that he couldn't really see anything.

So, forgetting his dignity, he climbed up a roadside sycamore tree in order to see Jesus. Perhaps to his surprise, when Jesus came to the spot he looked up and saw this little man perched in the tree. 'Zacchaeus,' he called (how *did* he know the man's name?), 'hurry and come down; for I must stay at your house today' (v. 5). Through a simple process of seeing and being seen—something that happens every waking moment of our everyday lives—a miracle of conversion was about to take place. The eyes of two of the unlikeliest of people, the thieving but rich tax collector and the honest but poor prophet, met in that moment. An invitation was offered—or, rather, an invitation was invited! Jesus asked himself to a meal and a bed at Zacchaeus' house. The little swindler hurried to climb down from the tree and was 'happy to welcome him' (v. 6). What, the bystanders must have wondered, was going on?

There had already been complaints from the straitlaced and orthodox that Jesus spent too much time hobnobbing with tax collectors and 'sinners'. For shame, he even 'ate with them' (15:2)! Now, in front of everyone, he was asking if he could dine and stay the night at the home of a chief tax collector who was locally notorious for dishonest dealing. Their problem was, they had not seen what Jesus saw in Zacchaeus; nor had they seen, sadly, what Zacchaeus obviously saw in Jesus.

Right at the start of Luke's Gospel, Jesus' messianic manifesto was set out, in words taken from Isaiah. Among its clauses was the statement that he had come to bring 'recovery of sight to the blind' (4:18). The disciples had seen people healed of physical blindness, but there is a stream of thought in the Gospels—explicit in John, if only implied in the other three—that the true recovery of sight to which Jesus was committed was spiritual. Until that moment up the sycamore tree, the eyes of Zacchaeus were closed to spiritual reality. Somewhere, somehow and at some point in his encounter with Jesus that began when their eyes met, those 'inner' eyes were opened.

What Zacchaeus then saw made him a changed man. His inward repentance was sealed by outward and visible restitution. Half of his possessions would go to the poor. Much of the rest would go to repaying fourfold anyone he had defrauded. No wonder Jesus said, 'Today salvation has come to this house, because he too is a son of Abraham' (19:9).

A reflection

The last words of this story encapsulate not only its message but the whole purpose of the coming of Jesus, in memorable and simple words: 'The Son of Man came to seek out and to save the lost' (v. 10). Sometimes, however, as Zacchaeus discovered, the 'lost' have to do a little bit of seeking themselves.

A poem : 'On Zacchaeus'

This poem has always been one of my favourites. It's by a 17th-century poet, Francis Quarles (1592–1644), and it tells the story of Zacchaeus with wit, style and no little spiritual perception.

Me thinks, I see, with what a busy haste,
Zacchaeus climb'd the Tree. But O how fast,
How full of speed, canst thou imagine (when
Our Saviour call'd) he powder'd down again!
He ne'er made trial if the boughs were sound,
Or rotten; nor how far 'twas to the ground:
There was no danger fear'd; At such a Call,
He'll venture nothing, that doth fear a fall;
Needs must he down, by such a Spirit driven;
Nor could he fall, unless he fall to Heaven:
Down came Zacchaeus, ravished from the Tree;
Bird that was shot ne'er dropt so quick as he.

SEEING CLEARLY

READ MARK 10:46–52.

Key verses: The blind man said to him, 'My teacher, let me see again.' Jesus said to him, 'Go, your faith has made you well'. Immediately he regained his sight and followed him on the way (vv. 51–52).

Having spent the night at the home of Zacchaeus, Jesus and the disciples took their leave and made their way out of Jericho—but one more incident would delay their departure. As they were leaving, Mark tells us, a blind beggar called Bartimaeus, who was sitting by the roadside begging (probably at one of the gates of the city), interrupted their progress. Zacchaeus couldn't see Jesus because he was short and the crowd was large. Bartimaeus couldn't see Jesus because he couldn't see. His ears picked up the commotion, though, and he heard the identity of the visitor: 'Jesus of Nazareth'.

The blind beggar must have heard tell of this prophet from Galilee and especially of his reputation as a healer. He wasn't going to let this one opportunity pass so he started shouting at the top of his voice, 'Jesus, Son of David, have mercy on me!' (v. 47).

His choice of title is interesting and perhaps decisive in what followed. It was the name chanted by the crowds as Jesus rode down the mount of Olives a few days later: 'Hosanna to the Son of David!' (Matthew 21:9). Those people, mostly Galileans, were quite clear about it: the prophet from Nazareth in Galilee was the Messiah, the promised one who would restore the kingdom of David. After all, they had seen the signs and healings, heard the words that came from his lips. Bartimaeus had no such experience: Jericho was far away from the towns and villages of Galilee where these wonderful things had happened. Yet, although he was physically blind, there seems to have been a degree of spiritual perception given to him that the other bystanders in Jericho missed. At any rate, he didn't hesitate to address Jesus in messianic language, for 'Son of David' could hardly mean anything less. Some inner prompting, or some stirring of faith or prophetic insight, seems to have told the blind man what the others around him failed to see. If the Messiah of God, no less, was passing by, then surely that above all was the moment to seek his attention: 'Have mercy on me!'

The crowd were not pleased with him, telling him to be quiet. Whether this was because they regarded his behaviour as unseemly or disorderly or because they were shocked by his messianic language we cannot know. Their remonstrances had the opposite effect, however. He cried out even more loudly, 'Son of David, have mercy on me!'

Jesus stopped in his tracks. 'Call him here,' he said, and they did. 'Get up, he is calling you', Bartimaeus was told (v. 49). The blind man threw off his cloak, sprang up and came to Jesus. For a moment they stood face to face. Jesus then asked him a simple, direct question: 'What do you want me to do for you?'

He had addressed exactly the same question a few days earlier, in precisely the same words, to James and John, the two disciples who had come to him privately and said that they wanted him to do for them whatever they asked (Mark 10:35–36). 'What do you want me to do for you?' Jesus asked them. What they wanted, as we have seen, was status—leading roles in his future kingdom. Gently at first, and then with a degree of impatience, he told them (and then the other ten) that they had got it all wrong. Places of honour were not on offer and, in any case, were not his to allocate. Those who would follow him must do what he did and make themselves servants of all.

Now, by the gate of Jericho, however, the question was answered very simply. 'What do you want me to do for you?' Bartimaeus didn't even have to think about it. 'My teacher (Rabbouni),' he said, 'let me see again.' The blind beggar had sensed that here was someone who could open eyes, even his. Indeed, his eyes had already been opened to a great truth apparently invisible to most of the crowd around him—that Jesus of Nazareth was more than a prophet; he was the Messiah of God. Now that spiritual vision was to be complemented by physical sight. Jesus said to him, 'Go; your faith has made you well', and immediately he received his sight and followed Jesus 'on the way'.

Once again, as with the grateful Samaritan leper, we see the distinction between a 'cure' and 'health'. Bartimaeus received more than simply his sight. He was made well, made whole—'saved', in religious language. Not only that, but he became a disciple, a follower of Jesus: 'he followed him on the way'. As with that Samaritan, the implication of those words would not have been lost on first-generation Christians, the 'people of the Way'. Now, along with various men and women who had thrown in their lot with Jesus—fishermen, tax collectors, former terrorists, wealthy women and some of dubious reputation—there was a man who was once blind but now, in every sense of the word, could see.

A reflection

'Open my eyes, so that I may behold wondrous things out of your law' (Psalm 119:18).

Day 17: Friday

NEW LIFE AT BETHANY

READ JOHN 11:17–44.

Key verses: Jesus said to her, 'I am the resurrection and the life. Those who believe in me, even though they die, will live, and everyone who lives and believes in me will never die' (vv. 25–26).

As Jesus and his followers set off from Jericho on the last stage of their journey to Jerusalem, they probably offered a strange sight. At the head, one imagines, there was Jesus himself, striding purposefully towards his destiny. Behind him, perhaps still a trifle reluctantly, would have been the Twelve, the 'apostles' or 'special messengers' whom he had chosen and appointed. Behind them may well have stretched quite a long line of less formally recognized disciples, men and women, including (it would be nice to think) a Samaritan who had once been a leper and Bartimaeus who had once been blind.

It may have been only 15 miles or so from Jericho to Jerusalem by the old road, which wound its way between cavernous cliffs and through rocky crevices, but it was uphill all the way and the territory through which they would pass was utterly inhospitable. Even today, the 'wilderness of Judea' looks like the surface of the moon, barren and rock-strewn, baked hard in the relentless heat of the sun. As most of the party were convinced that Jesus was walking straight into arrest and execution, with their own fates perhaps determined largely by his, it would be understandable if they made their way onwards and upwards with mixed feelings.

It may well be, however, that they approached Jerusalem by way of a detour. It is often hard to harmonize the account of Jesus' movements in John's Gospel with the story as the other three accounts present it, but John seems to suggest that Jesus left the Jordan valley on hearing of the death of his friend Lazarus, the brother of Mary and Martha, and went (after a delay of four days, for some reason) to their home at Bethany, a few miles outside the city. This home features in the other Gospels, too, as a place of refuge and rest for Jesus at different times in his ministry (see, for example, Mark 11:12; Luke 10:38–42). Bethany would certainly have made a convenient base for a group of people visiting Jerusalem, although, as we shall see, John suggests a further place of refuge near the city during this dangerous and difficult time.

Whatever we make of the chronology and the geography, it would be hard to write of this last fateful journey without reference to the intriguing and mysterious story of the raising of Lazarus from the dead. This is the last of the miraculous 'signs' in John's Gospel, events that 'revealed his glory' (2:11), until the last and greatest of them all, the resurrection of Jesus.

Some have seen the raising of Lazarus as a prefiguring of the resurrection, others as a vivid demonstration of a truth that Jesus had already expressed in words: 'just as the Father raises the dead and gives them life, so also the Son gives life to whomsoever he wishes' (John 5:21).

The reasons for an apparent reluctance on the part of some scholars to take this account at face value—that is, as a straight-forward report of something that actually happened—are its complete absence from the other three Gospels (even though the family at Bethany was known to the writers) and the feeling that, like so much of this amazing Gospel, there is clearly more to this than meets the eye. That seems to be unduly sceptical, though. There are many possible reasons why the other Gospel writers have omitted this story, the most obvious being that, at the time when those earlier Gospels were being written, Lazarus was still alive and it would be embarrassing (or possibly even physically dangerous) to draw attention to him. We may assume that by the time John's Gospel appeared, 20 or more years later, Lazarus, Mary and Martha were no longer alive.

We may readily agree that there is more to this story than meets the eye without subscribing to the view that it is no more than some kind of spiritual allegory. The people named are characters familiar to us from all the Gospels; the location is a known one; the dialogues (with the disciples and with Mary and Martha) have the ring of truth; and John's deduction that it was this miracle—performed almost on the doorstep of the temple—that finally drove the Jewish Council to decide that Jesus must be put to death seems logical, if chilling.

It also fits quite well into the chronology of the synoptic Gospels (Matthew, Mark and Luke) to see the disciples and Jesus arriving from Jericho (the Jordan valley, in broad terms) and, needing a place to stay during their visit to Jerusalem, finding it with these close friends of Jesus. The strange element is the apparently deliberate delay in arriving at Bethany (John 11:5), so that by the time Jesus came to his grave Lazarus had been dead four days and, as Martha put it, there would be the stench of decomposition already (v. 39). Nevertheless, Jesus went ahead, having the stone over the tomb's entrance removed, calling the dead man from his grave and ordering the bystanders to take the funeral wrappings off him as he staggered out.

Jesus' actions complemented his words to Martha: 'I am the resurrection and the life' (v. 25). Eternal life, for those who believe in him, does not have to wait for the great day of resurrection. It is now, wherever Jesus is. He is resurrection himself, the one who has God-given authority to 'give life to whomsoever he wishes' (John 5:21). So now he gives life to dead Lazarus and offers it to those who believe in him, *whether they are physically dead or alive*. That, surely, is the meaning of the statement, 'those who believe in me, even though they die, will live, and whoever lives and believes in me will never die'.

There is a dramatic paradox at the opening of most funeral services, for as the coffin is carried in, with a dead human body inside it, the minister is saying that there is no death for those who believe in Jesus—and saying it in these very categorical words. I sometimes wish that I had the courage to complete the whole saying and add the challenge of Jesus to Martha: 'Do you believe this?' (v. 26). In the face of the visible evidence of death, we express our faith in Christ's victory over it—and that victory is now, in the sense that it has already been won for us. All that remains is for the mopping-up process to be complete, and then we shall see that the 'last enemy', as Paul calls death, has been finally defeated (1 Corinthians 15:26).

This 'sign' of the raising of Lazarus is indeed a fitting prologue to the narrative of the death and resurrection of Jesus. 'In him was life,' says John of 'the Word', Jesus (1:4), and even a cruel crucifixion could not extinguish it. More than that, the life that Jesus has is resurrection life, and those who follow him share in that life too. Yes, there is more in this story than meets the eye, but it is all highly relevant to what follows. There was new life at Bethany, and it is new life that will burst forth from the tomb a week or two later on Easter morning.

A reflection

'Do you believe this?' Jesus asked Martha—to which she replied, slightly obliquely, that she believed that Jesus was the Messiah, the Son of God. Presumably the implication of her words was that the Messiah of God could be expected to speak the truth, and if he said so, then she believed it. She might have a few difficulties with 'this' (the notion that Jesus was the resurrection, or that those who were dead would live through him) but she had no problems with 'him'.

Day 18: Saturday

THE ANOINTING OF JESUS

READ JOHN 12:1–7.

Key verse: Jesus said, 'Leave her alone. She bought it so that she might keep it for the day of my burial' (v. 7).

From Bethany, it would seem, if we follow John's record, that Jesus withdrew to a town called Ephraim, 'in the region near the wilderness' (11:54). This place is sometimes known as Ephron and there is a modern town on the site called el-Taiyibeh. It's about 20 miles from Jerusalem, to the north-west of the city, on the edge of the Judean hills—a good place for a hideaway in the light of the public frenzy which, John tells us, followed the raising of Lazarus. The temple authorities had finally decided that the time had come to seek the arrest of Jesus and let it be known that they would welcome information about his whereabouts. The withdrawal to Ephraim was the immediate, if temporary, response of Jesus, who would doubtless have said that his hour had not yet come.

So Jesus and the disciples waited in their desert safe-house until six days before the Passover, but then went back to Mary and Martha's home at Bethany for a dinner at which Lazarus was an honoured (and no doubt surprised) guest. During the meal, which Martha had prepared, Mary took some costly perfume and with it anointed the feet of Jesus, wiping them with her hair. And, we are told, 'the house was filled with the fragrance of the perfume' (v. 3).

John tells us that Judas objected to this, on the grounds of waste: the perfume could have been sold for 300 denarii (almost a year's wages) and the money given to the poor. The parenthesis that follows is John's rather bitter comment: 'He said this not because he cared about the poor, but because he was a thief; he kept the common purse' (v. 6). John may have been privy to more inside knowledge than the other disciples, but the fact remains that Mark ascribes the comment about waste and the poor to 'some who were there', and Matthew collectively to 'the disciples', rather than exclusively to Judas (Mark 14:4; Matthew 26:8).

Every Gospel includes a story of Jesus being anointed in this way, by a woman in the course of a meal. Matthew, Mark and John set it at this point in the narrative and explicitly tie it in to the notion of anointing for burial. Mark and Matthew, however, place it in the house of 'Simon the leper' while John, as we see here, sets the scene in the home of Lazarus, Mary and Martha. All three give the place as Bethany. Luke seems to relate a different story altogether, at the home of an unnamed Pharisee, which has a completely different theme, about repentance, love and forgiveness.

Whatever the details, Matthew, Mark and John are agreed that the significance of this anointing was in its association with funeral ritual. Jesus saw the woman's action as prefiguring his imminent death and burial, thus putting into powerful visual form the prophetic words he had spoken so often to the disciples, that he was to be delivered into the hands of wicked men in Jerusalem and killed.

The scene clearly shocked them, and the implication of Mark and Matthew's account (notice the important preposition 'then' at the beginning of Matthew 26:14 and Mark 14:10) is that this event finally persuaded Judas to offer the high priests the information they wanted. We shall examine the role of Judas more closely in a later chapter.

Apparently a 'great crowd' (John 12:9) had gathered at the house in Bethany, not just to see Jesus but also to get a glimpse of the man who had been raised from the dead, Lazarus. According to John, this persuaded the chief priests that it would be necessary to put not only Jesus to death but Lazarus as well—a rather bizarre notion, given recent events. Because of the miracle at Bethany, 'many Jews' (v. 11) were believing in Jesus, and if this rebellious young teacher were to gather a large following it would be disastrous, provoking the Romans into a pre-emptive takeover of the nation's institutions. As it was put at a meeting of the Council, 'If we let him go on like this, everyone will believe in him, and the Romans will come and destroy both our holy place [the Temple] and our nation' (11:48). This prompted the high priest, Caiaphas, to argue that it was better 'to have one man die for the people than to have the whole nation destroyed' (v. 50). John adds a comment of his own: 'Being high priest that year he prophesied that Jesus was about to die for the nation, and not for the nation only, but to gather into one the dispersed children of God' (vv. 51–52).

It would seem that these few days spent at Bethany and Ephraim were the final stage of the journey of Jesus and the disciples to Jerusalem. Jesus was set on his purpose. Nothing would deflect him from what he knew to be his divine calling. As for the disciples, we can assume a rare mix of emotions. Perhaps there was a sense of excitement: at last, something was going to happen, and they were used to Jesus being in complete control of events. On the other hand, he had told them himself what lay ahead, and it sounded ominous and terrifying. Yet still they followed, carried along by their faith in him as Messiah and their experience of his past triumphs. Surely the man who raised the dead could not himself be put to death?

A reflection

Whether it is a fair interpretation of the words of Caiaphas or John's later insight, it is a profound truth that in putting Jesus to death the temple authorities would bring about the death of one man not only for their nation, but to 'gather into one the dispersed children of God'. They did not know it, but they were helping to fulfil a far more profound and far-reaching plan than the one they were hatching in the temple.

FOLLOWING THE GOOD SHEPHERD

READ JOHN 10:2–5.

Key verse: 'He goes ahead of them, and the sheep follow him because they know his voice' (v. 4).

Shepherds were a familiar and essential part of life in biblical times, but it is possible for readers today to romanticize their role. David was a shepherd as a boy, of course, called from the hills to be anointed by the prophet Samuel and eventually to become Israel's greatest king. Yet the fact is that shepherds generally were not well regarded; indeed, they were almost social outcasts, being unable through the nature of their work to fulfil their religious obligations or join fully in the normal life of the community. It is that which gives added point to the story of the boy David—and to the involvement of the hillside shepherds in the angels' announcement of the birth of Jesus. These are examples of God choosing what is 'low and despised in the world' to shame the worldly-wise, as Paul put it (1 Corinthians 1:27–28).

In a similar paradox, the best kings of Israel and Judah were seen as 'shepherds' of their people, and Isaiah even depicts the Lord God as a shepherd, feeding his flock and gathering the lambs in his arms (40:11).

It is really no surprise, then, that the Messiah Jesus is also able to see his role as a shepherd to his people. The shepherd guards the flock, acts as a gate to the fold to keep the true flock in and the would-be predators out. He feeds them and defends them, even to the extent of laying down his life for them (John 10:11). He knows his sheep by name, and they know (recognize) him (vv. 3–4). False shepherds—'thieves and bandits'—come to steal and destroy. The good shepherd has come 'that they may have life, and have it abundantly' (v. 10).

Who are these fortunate sheep, members of so privileged a flock, with such a caring and loving shepherd? They are those who 'follow him' (v. 4). It still comes as something of a surprise to visitors to the Holy Land to see that shepherds lead their flocks. We are more accustomed to shepherds bringing up the rear, often with a couple of sheepdogs to assist—or nowadays seated on an all-terrain vehicle. The sheep in the Middle East follow, because the way may be dangerous and difficult, and only the shepherd knows where the good pasture and still waters are to be found.

To follow the shepherd, even sheep have to obey simple but vital rules. They must keep him in sight. They must not follow whims or fancies of their own, wandering off and 'straying from his ways like lost sheep', as the old prayer says. They must attend to his voice, both to know that they are following the true shepherd and to pick up any warning or guidance that his words may imply. What is true for sheep is true for the people of Christ's flock today and in every age. We must keep him in sight, not wandering from the pathway, not following our own whims and fancies but attending to his voice. By doing that, we shall be true followers and privileged members of his flock.

A reflection

There is nothing exclusive about Christ's flock. He has 'other sheep that do not belong to this fold' (v. 16)—Gentiles, perhaps, or God-fearers of other cultures and traditions. 'I must bring them also,' he says, 'and they will listen to my voice. So there will be one flock, one shepherd.' Any and

*all who listen to his voice and follow him are members of his flock—
valued, loved, protected, saved.*

Part Three

THE DESTINATION REACHED

Day 20: Monday

DOWN THE MOUNT
OF OLIVES

READ MARK 11:1–11.

Key verse: 'Hosanna! Blessed is the one who comes in the name of the Lord! Blessed is the coming kingdom of our ancestor David! Hosanna in the highest heaven!' (vv. 9–10).

Either direct from Jericho (according to Matthew, Mark and Luke) or by way of a detour and a few days' rest at Bethany and Ephraim, Jesus and his band of followers have finally reached their destination, the holy city of Jerusalem. As they came to the Mount of Olives, it would have stretched out before their eyes in the spring sunshine: palaces, houses, narrow streets, markets and, dominating the skyline, the magnificent temple built by Herod the Great—a vast edifice into which you could have comfortably fitted half a dozen cathedrals and more.

They had approached the city from the south and passed through what are now the southern suburbs, Bethphage and Bethany. The Gospels are not very bothered about precise dating of events, so we can only estimate that this would have been a week or perhaps ten days before the Passover. Jesus told two of his disciples to go into a nearby village where they would see a colt tied up, an animal that had never been ridden. They were to untie it and bring it to him. If anyone were to ask, understandably, why they were doing this, the answer was to be that 'the Lord needs it and will send it back here immediately' (v. 3). Whether this suggests a preplanned arrangement or a spontaneous decision is left to the reader to decide, although the details of the colt's whereabouts and condition suggest the former rather than the latter.

At any rate, the task was fulfilled and the beast was brought to Jesus. Cloaks were laid on it (no such sophistication as a saddle) and Jesus mounted it and rode off, followed by the cheering crowd of Galileans, along the path down the Mount of Olives towards the city gates.

It's worth noticing, in passing, that the animal bearing Jesus was a young colt that had not been broken in. I remember being told, many years ago, of a jockey who came with some friends to a church service near Newmarket. It was Palm Sunday and this passage was read. Thereafter he seemed incapable of concentrating on anything in the service, but as soon as the blessing was pronounced he turned to his friends and said, 'Did you hear what the chap read from up there? That Jesus was some rider! Fancy getting on a young animal that had never been broken in and then riding it through all that noise and kerfuffle, people waving palm branches and shouting in its ears! I'd like to know a bit more about him!'

Despite all that (and it's amazing how many times we can read a story like that and not see so astonishing an achievement), the colt and its rider made their way down the hillside. The shouts of the disciples must have echoed across the valley towards the city walls: 'Hosanna!' This Hebrew word, which they would have picked up from Psalm 118:25, literally means 'Save, we pray'. Psalm 118 was recited during the feast of Tabernacles and had assumed clear messianic overtones, so the disciples undoubtedly knew precisely what they were doing. In case there was any doubt about it, however, they clarified the call: 'Blessed is the one who comes in the name of the Lord! Blessed is the coming kingdom of our ancestor David!' Then they cut down palm branches (see John 12:13), which would have recalled to those who knew Jewish history their use in the victory procession 130 years earlier, when the citadel of Jerusalem was recaptured by Simon Maccabeus.

We may add one more detail. It was no accident or matter of convenience that Jesus came riding on a donkey's foal, but a direct fulfilment of Zechariah's prophecy: 'Lo, your king comes to you; triumphant and victorious is he, humble and riding on a donkey, on a colt, the foal of a donkey' (9:9).

With all this going on, it is no surprise that a wider crowd gathered from within the city, asking, 'Who is this?' The crowd of disciples knew the answer and doubtless said it with some pride: 'This is the prophet Jesus from Nazareth in Galilee' (Matthew 21:11). It's also not surprising that the turmoil drew some Pharisees and scribes to investigate or perhaps to seek ammunition for a future prosecution of Jesus. They said to him, 'Teacher, order your disciples to stop' (Luke 19:39): in other words, 'dissociate yourself from these messianic claims, and also from the notion that you are about to set up a kingdom here'—a threat that the Roman authorities could not possibly ignore. The reply of Jesus was simple, dignified and shocking: 'I tell you, if these were silent, the stones would shout out' (v. 40).

This was the last such moment of triumph, at least until Easter morning. The band of disciples who had followed him from Galilee were obviously in high spirits and were undoubtedly joined by others who had been touched by the ministry of Jesus, including the lonely figure of Judas Iscariot, the only non-Galilean among the Twelve. For a few wonderful moments they may have thought that the kingdom of God was about to appear in Jerusalem itself. Surely even the sophisticates of the city would see that this was no ordinary prophet, this no everyday arrival at their gates. Surely now the longed-for breakthrough was at hand. They could not doubt that God was with Jesus. Surely his power was greater than that of the corrupt temple hierarchy or the pagan rule of Rome?

A reflection

Most of us, at some time or other, have experienced moments when the truth seemed so crystal clear and the glory of God so real that we felt buoyed up, lifted almost out of ourselves. There is no harm—indeed, much good—in reflecting on those times and nourishing their memory, especially when setbacks occur and doubts begin to creep in. After all, the same God who was with the crowd swarming gleefully down the Mount of Olives was also with many of the same people as they clustered sorrowfully on the slope of a different hill, Golgotha, just a few days later.

THE DEN OF ROBBERS

READ MARK 11:15–19.

Key verse: 'Is it not written, "My house shall be called a house of prayer for all the nations"? But you have made it a den of robbers' (v. 17).

There had been a temple on the same site in Jerusalem for nearly a thousand years. It had been repaired or rebuilt and now, in the case of the one that lay before Jesus and his party, completely and spectacularly redeveloped. Over the centuries the view had constantly changed, but each of the temple buildings stood on the same temple mount, the place where it was believed that Abraham was called to sacrifice his son Isaac. The site had been purchased by King David for this specific purpose (see 2 Samuel 24:24–25; 2 Chronicles 3:1).

The temple of Herod, which represented a total redevelopment of the whole site, had not yet been completed at the time of Jesus. In fact, it was finally finished in AD64, just in time for the Romans to raze it to the ground at the end of the Jewish Revolution in AD70. Since then, the Jewish people have had no temple and hence no sacrifices and no priesthood. Even unfinished, however, it was a splendid edifice, with various courts (for Gentiles, for Jewish women, for Jewish men and finally for the priests and then the high priest) surrounding the Holy Place and the innermost sanctuary, which was closed off with a heavy curtain and entered only on the Day of Atonement by the high priest.

The temple was consequently something of a tourist attraction, in first-century terms, with Jews visiting it from far-flung corners of the Mediterranean lands and many Gentiles also coming to see what they could of its wonders. This all led to a flourishing trade, especially in birds and beasts for sacrifices and in exchanging Roman and other money for the special temple coinage. The stalls and booths of the sellers and money changers filled the outside courts, and business was doubtless brisk—especially in the week leading up to Passover.

As Jesus and the disciples, perhaps still flushed with the enthusiasm of the triumphal entry into the city, entered the temple courts under the great arch with a magnificent carving of a vine on it, they might well have been taken aback at the sight before them. Most of them had surely seen the merchants and money changers there before, but somehow, at this moment, it seemed so inappropriate, so far from their vision of the coming kingdom. It was visible and audible proof of all that Jesus had taught them about the corruption of much that passed for religion.

If the view shocked the disciples, it inflamed Jesus. With shouts of anger and disgust, he began to overturn the market tables, scattering live animals and coins in every direction. 'My house shall be called a house of prayer for all the nations,' he told them, quoting from Isaiah 56:7—'but you have made it a den of robbers'. We may wonder what the bystanders and visitors made of it all— the crash of tables being overturned, the shouts of Jesus, the chaos of fleeing birds and animals and the cascade of coins across the outer court of the temple. This was hardly an anonymous entry on to the public scene in the city. Instead, it almost seems as if Jesus was deliberately drawing attention to his arrival and to the introduction of a completely new approach to worship and prayer. The temple, known familiarly to Jews as 'the Father's House', was for prayer, not trading, and its courts, far from existing to exclude people from the presence of God, were intended in his vision of things to offer a place of prayer for 'all the nations'.

As a boy of twelve, Jesus had stayed behind in this very building when the rest of the family set off on their way back to Nazareth, so that he could sit at the feet of the teachers of the Law and ask them questions. Apparently he also answered some, to the amazement of the hearers. On that occasion he called the place 'my Father's house' (Luke 2:49), and perhaps, from that event 20 years earlier, he had come to see the temple as a sacred place where men and women, young and old, could find the truth of God. As he grew up, he would certainly have learnt of the corruption and compromise that had become the hallmarks of the temple clique.

The Essenes, from their monastic settlement at Qumran, and John the Baptist in the Jordan valley made no secret of their contempt for the priestly hierarchy of the time. Desperate not to upset the pagan occupiers (for fear that they would lose their beloved temple and, even more seriously, their toehold on any kind of power), they had trimmed and tacked with every little breeze from Pilate's palace. They had supported the quisling court of the Herods and managed to gain the reluctant acquiescence of most of the Pharisees and Sadducees. Doubtless, some of their number worked from the premise that something was better than nothing, and that under Roman rule that was the stark choice before them. We certainly know that not all the members of the Council, the Sanhedrin, were entirely happy with their tactics, but short of an armed uprising, with precious little chance of success, what could they do?

All of this may help to explain why the actions of Jesus—in the temple and elsewhere—were a cause of so much anxiety and fear to the temple priests. For them, he was probably just an irresponsible troublemaker who could not see the logical consequence of his crazed actions. Would-be messiahs were two a penny at the time, but the uneasy co-existence they had negotiated with the Romans seemed, to them, priceless.

It went further than that, of course. There is more than a suggestion in the Gospels and in other documents that the temple hierarchy were adept at feathering their own nests and had certainly raised nepotism to an art form. There was a high priestly 'family' and the succession was always carefully predetermined. This was not exactly the picture of the priesthood that the levitical laws had been designed to achieve. The temple authorities, in other words, may have had sound pragmatic reasons for fearing the activities of Jesus and his supporters, but their motives were tainted, to say the least.

By the time Jesus and his friends withdrew to the house at Bethany for the night, it would be fair to say that the whole city had been alerted to their presence. Jesus could no longer be dismissed as yet another half-baked prophet from the sticks. This man had authority, courage and a clear-cut manifesto. As Mark puts it, 'The whole crowd was spellbound by his teaching' (11:18).

A reflection

To do good sometimes—perhaps often—involves also being ready to oppose evil.

Day 22: Wednesday

THE STRANGE INCIDENT
OF THE FIG TREE

READ MARK 11:12–14, 20–24.

Key verse: Then Peter remembered and said to him, 'Rabbi, look! The fig tree that you cursed has withered.' Jesus answered them, 'Have faith in God' (vv. 21–22).

I remember, as a teenager, being taught Religious Knowledge by a charming but convinced communist. On one occasion he invited us to think about Jesus as a normal, fallible human being and chose two examples. One was the incident we were considering yesterday, when, with a degree of violence, Jesus drove the merchants and money changers out of the temple—using a whip made of cords, John tells us (2:15). The second was this strange business of the cursing of the fig tree. Our teacher suggested that in both cases Jesus had 'lost it'—justifiably, in his view, where the agents of capitalism were plying their evil trade, but petulantly and inexcusably in the case of the fig tree. For him, it was simply a tantrum brought on by the fact that Jesus had hoped to find some juicy figs for breakfast and was disappointed. Stamping his foot (as it were), he cursed the little tree: 'May no one ever eat fruit from you again' (Mark 11:14).

I was fascinated by my teacher's argument, but unconvinced, although it was a long while before I came to see that this incident, like so many in the Gospels, could not simply be taken at face value. There had to be a reason why Jesus, who had never exhibited anything remotely like petulance before, should suddenly take it out on a fig tree—and especially one that could not be expected to be bearing figs because, as Mark carefully tells us, 'it was not the season for figs' (v. 13). Presumably a good countryman like Jesus would have known that too.

Mark puts the first part of this story before the 'cleansing' of the temple; and the final part (the revelation that the fig tree had in fact withered and died) after it. That placing is unlikely to have been accidental, which suggests that the temple incident has some relevance to our understanding of the fig tree story.

The prophet Jeremiah had warned that the king of Judah, 'his officials, [and] the remnant of Jerusalem who remain in this land' would be like a basket of bad figs—'a disgrace, a byword, a taunt and a curse in all the places where I shall drive them' (24:8–9). Whether this prophecy was specifically in mind here or not, the idea of Israel as a 'fruitful' nation runs right through the Hebrew scriptures (our Old Testament), as does the recurrent warning about the perils of being 'fruitless'. Both of these incidents—the temple cleansing and the cursed fig tree—are in fact about fruitfulness, about the people of the covenant living in the way the Lord God required and showing to the surrounding nations the 'fruits' of true religion.

What had happened in the temple was the corruption or distortion of true religion, but it represented a more widespread distortion that had crept into the life of the nation. This distortion was a major theme of the teaching of Jesus (as it was of the Essenes and, at their best, of the Pharisees) and here, in action and in parable, the point is rammed home. Certainly the disciples were never likely to forget it—the spectacular scene in the temple matched by the sight of the withered fig tree, no longer capable of bearing fruit.

It seems clear that this was the intention of Jesus. He knew, as he approached the fig tree the previous morning, that it was unlikely that a fig tree in full leaf would be bearing fruit: 'he went to see whether *perhaps* he would find anything on it' (Mark 11:13). He also knew that 'it was not the season for figs'. Nevertheless, looking at this tree, so proud of its leaves but so lacking in fruit, the parallel with the spiritual state of the covenant people must have seemed too good a teaching point to miss. 'May no one ever eat fruit of you again' then becomes not so much a curse as a judgment: this is what things will be like for the privileged people of God's choice if they continue to display the outward signs of life but lack the fruit that is evidence of its reality.

The day after Jesus had spoken to the fig tree, the startled disciples watched as he effected a rather similar visual aid in the temple courts. The traders had turned a house of prayer into a den of robbers. This was 'religion', but of a corrupt, distorted kind, showing nothing of the fruit that Jesus had often taught about— the fruit by which the true people of the kingdom would be identified. As he had told them, 'Figs are not gathered from thorns' (Luke 6:43–45).

The problem went deeper, though, than simply a handful of traders and money changers in the temple courts. It was endemic in the life of a nation that had taken a wrong turning, and the incident of the fig tree broadens the picture. Without repentance and new life, the 'fig tree' of Israel would never produce fruit. Its destiny would be perpetual barrenness.

So, as they passed the same spot the next day on their walk from Bethany into the city, the disciples noticed that the harmless little fig tree had 'withered away to its roots' (Mark 11:20)—probably the victim of the scorching sun or an acute shortage of water. But the point was made: 'Rabbi, look! The fig tree that you cursed has withered' (v. 21). The picture would have remained as vividly in their memories as the scene in the temple the previous day.

The response of Jesus to their surprise (and perhaps shock) was not what we might have expected. He didn't offer an exposition of the sins of this 'faithless and perverse generation' (Luke 9:41) as he had often done in the past, but instead directed his words at the disciples themselves: 'Have faith in God'. That was where their contemporaries had gone wrong. They had limited the power and authority of God and put their trust in human powers and authorities. They had exchanged the realities of faith for the tawdry trappings of religion. So Jesus warned his disciples not to fall into the same trap of faithlessness, but to believe in the God who can 'move mountains' (Mark 11:23). If Roman rule was the problem, or a corrupt temple hierarchy, let them be sure that God was greater than the emperor and far, far greater than the high priests. The 'mountains' may vary, but the people of his covenant must have faith that he can move them—yes, even remove the hated conquerors and replace them with a new and godly kingdom.

A reflection

Corrupt and tawdry religion did not cease with the destruction of the temple 40 years later. It is still with us, both outwardly, in the kind of religion that lines the pockets or boosts the status of its proponents, and inwardly in the kind of personal religion that is strong on display but weak on fruit. Probably none of us is faultless in one respect or the other.

Day 23: Thursday

THE REJECTED CORNERSTONE

READ MATTHEW 21:42–46.

Key verse: The stone that the builders rejected has become the cornerstone; this was the Lord's doing, and it is amazing in our eyes (v. 42).

It seems that Jesus and the disciples followed a fairly set routine during the days between their arrival in Jerusalem and the Passover. They spent each evening at Bethany, in the home of Lazarus, Martha and Mary, and then each morning walked down the Mount of Olives and across the valley before making their way up into the temple area of the city. There the disciples watched and wondered while Jesus taught them—sometimes (though not often) in homilies or discourses, more often by example, illustration or answered question. The strange incident of the fig tree, which we reflected on yesterday, is one example, but there are many others, including the poor widow and her two 'mites' willingly given to God (Mark 12:41–44), a question from a scribe about Roman coinage (Matthew 22:15–22), and the incident we are looking at today. In fact, several times Jesus used the temple building itself as a vast teaching aid.

We know that the disciples were little short of awestruck at the temple's magnificence and scale. 'Look, Teacher,' they said to him once, 'what large stones and what large buildings!' (Mark 13:1).

For men who had grown up in rural Galilee, with its single-storey houses and unpretentious architecture, all of this would have seemed vast and improbable. They must have seen it on occasions before, but perhaps neither so closely nor in the company of so perceptive and knowing a guide as Jesus was. The pinnacles and domes soared up into the blue April sky over their heads. The great walls closed them in. There were carvings and fine curtains, arches and steps and windows. This, surely, was a building fit for the Almighty God it professed to honour. Yet their teacher seemed less than impressed, critical of the splendour and quick to tell them that one day soon it would all be reduced to rubble.

On this occasion, as they walked, someone in their number must have pointed out a discarded cornerstone (or it may have been a keystone). This is a major stone that locks together sections of masonry. Without it, the walls would fall and the roof cave in, so the cornerstone needs to be well chosen and perfectly fitted. Perhaps this cornerstone was lying on the ground waiting to be removed by the builders and replaced by a better one. If that were so, it would explain why Jesus was moved to quote from Psalm 118:22–23: 'The stone that the builders rejected has become the chief cornerstone. This is the Lord's doing; it is marvellous in our eyes.'

At any rate, the image of the rejected stone which was actually the ideal one for the purpose fitted in well with the most recurrent theme of his teaching during this last week of his life. He was being—in effect, already had been—rejected by the very people to whom the Father had sent him. For all the noisy enthusiasm of those early days in Galilee—the crowds, the miracles and healings, the teaching, even the feeding of the five thousand—those people had not seen, as this little band of disciples had done, that the Messiah of God was in their midst. Through spiritual blindness, apathy or fear, they acquiesced in his rejection. They stood by and watched as their religious leaders formally denied his claims to messiahship and conspired to have him put to death. As John succinctly puts it, 'He came to his own home, and his own people did not accept him' (1:11).

The teaching ministry of Jesus, as we have seen, took a significant change of emphasis after Caesarea Philippi. Once the Twelve had affirmed their belief in Jesus as God's Messiah, almost all of his attention was turned on to them. He had come, he once said, for 'the lost sheep of the house of Israel' (Matthew 10:6), but the lost sheep had decided to stay lost. Here were the faithful few who had chosen the hard and narrow path of following him, who had 'stood by him in his trials' (Luke 22:28). So the last months of his ministry were devoted almost entirely to confirming the disciples' faith and informing their minds. Soon, as he knew but they seemed so reluctant to believe, he would be gone and they would be left behind. The work of the kingdom, its mission, its ministry, would then be in their hands. There was no better way to spend the time he had remaining than to strengthen them.

Part of that instruction and strengthening had to do with their own responsibility in the future. If the people of the covenant had rejected their Messiah, then this little band of men and women— all of them, at this stage, also people of the covenant, Jewish both by race and religion—must bear the responsibility of letting the world know of his momentous coming. The Twelve were 'apostles', special messengers of the kingdom that the Messiah Jesus had inaugurated. The others would be witnesses, those who had 'seen his glory, the glory as of the Father's only Son' (John 1:14) and would share in the task of carrying his message to the whole world.

They would also need to understand the cruel implications for the people of historic Israel. The rejection of the one whom God had sent to them was no light matter. There would be consequences, sad and bitter, expressed here by Jesus in vivid terms: 'The kingdom of God will be taken away from you and given to a people that produces the fruits of the kingdom' (Matthew 21:43). We need to be clear about the nature of the two groups identified here. It is too simple to say that they are, on the one hand, 'the Jews' and, on the other, 'Gentile Christians'. After all, the first agents of the kingdom were all Jews, and so were all the founding figures of the Church of Christ—Peter, Paul, James, John and the other apostles. However, membership of that kingdom was no longer a matter of natural birth or race, but of faith in Jesus, the Son of God. Both Jews and Gentiles who recognized the Messiah Jesus and received him would constitute the new people of God. The apostle Peter's first letter puts it in striking (and largely Old Testament) language: having picked up the symbolic language of the rejected cornerstone (2:7) he goes on, 'But you [that is, the Christians scattered across the Middle East: see 1:1] are a chosen race, a royal priesthood, a holy nation, God's own people' (2:9).

The sad and bitter consequences that would follow the rejection of the Messiah were spelt out by Jesus later during this fateful week in Jerusalem. Here he simply takes the metaphor of the rejected stone and turns it, as we might say, upside down. The discarded cornerstone, massive but unwanted, will prove to be a heavy burden for those who have rejected it. Some will trip over it, as if it were a stumbling block. Others, more severely, will find that it falls on them, crushing them with its weight.

The cornerstone intended by God to hold the house together will, for those who discard it, become the stone that destroys them as it brings the edifice crashing down. The 'edifice' may have been the nation of Israel itself, cruelly dispersed across the nations after the abortive revolution against the Romans 40 years later, or it may have been the corrupt and compromised religious establishment of the day. They—the chief priests, the Council, even the Roman governor—thought that they were judging the claims of a would-be Messiah; in fact, the Messiah himself was judging them. They might see themselves as discarding an un-wanted stone; in fact, the stone they were discarding would be their judgment—and, sadly, that of their people. It would also, Jesus claimed, become the cornerstone of a new temple, not built with hands—a building made of the 'living stones' of God's new people (1 Peter 2:5).

A reflection

The Hebrew Scriptures often talk of God as a rock on which his people could build their security. As Jesus taught the people in a parable (Matthew 7:24–25), it is those who build their lives on a foundation of rock who stand firm in the time of trial.

Day 24: Friday

THE REALLY POOR
AND THE TRULY RICH

READ LUKE 20:45–47; 21:1–4.

Key verse: 'She out of her poverty has put in all she had to live on' (21:4).

During the days leading up to Passover, the temple courts saw quite a lot of Jesus and his disciples. Jesus used the building as a magnificent visual aid, but also, by the nature of the place and its multifarious uses, it was a wonderful place to observe people (especially those going about their religious obligations) and learn lessons from the observation. In today's passage, two pictures are drawn, and it can hardly be accidental that Matthew sets them alongside each other, as though inviting us to compare and contrast them.

The first is a warning addressed to 'his disciples' but 'in the hearing of all the people' (20:45). For the disciples it was a lesson to be learnt about true and false religion; for the people it may well have been a public indicator of where Jesus stood in relation to the scribes, the teachers of the law. The language is strong—vituperative, even—but then nothing offended Jesus more than bogus religious devotion. All through the Gospels, his most powerful invective is directed at those he calls 'hypocrites'—literally, 'play actors'.

The scribes (often linked with the Pharisees, but not in this passage) were the teachers or, more precisely, the interpreters of the

Jewish law. When you read the long sections of Exodus, Leviticus and Deuteronomy that set out the moral and ceremonial law (which Jewish tradition equated with the law delivered by God to Israel at Sinai), it seems hard to credit that in later centuries it would be deemed necessary to add to this a mountain of elucidatory material. Yet that is what had happened. The scribes presided over a massive industry of legal interpretation and application. Some of it was what we might call case law, some was based on precedent and much simply sprang from a desire on the part of these ecclesiastical lawyers to extract the last possible scrap of power from their knowledge of the fine print.

From this they enjoyed (if that is the right word) a high standing in society. They guarded the very heart of the Jewish faith. Their decisions were binding and respected. Through their knowledge of the scriptures and of legal precedent, they were able to invoke what they claimed were divine sanctions against those who challenged their rulings. Jesus warned his followers about them: it was, he said, all about outward show, about lording it round the town in long robes, being treated deferentially by inferior citizens and getting the best places in the synagogue and at banquets. How did they earn this respect? They said long prayers, certainly, but they also 'devoured widows' houses' (20:47)—a reference, probably, to various rules and laws relating to property left by a widow who had no surviving family. Jesus' judgment is severe. The scribes may do rather well now, but in the end 'they will receive the greater condemnation'.

The next incident is linked by the phrase 'looking up' (21:1). As Jesus ended his scathing words about the purveyors of false religion, his eye caught a practitioner of the true kind. Dotted around the Court of the Women, rather like collecting boxes in our cathedrals, were trumpet-shaped receptacles for alms. One must have been nearby and, as rich people were putting their generous gifts into it, he saw a poor widow come up and put in two tiny copper coins (the 'mites' of the King James Version). Jesus drew his disciples' attention to this, and then observed that she had put in more than all the others. They had simply given a part of what they had in abundance, but she, he said, had put in 'all she had to live on' (v. 4). Many of the rich people mentioned in the Gospels clung to their tawdry wealth at all costs: think of the rich man and the beggar (Luke 16:19–31), or the rich young ruler (Matthew 19:16–22), or the rich man who was going to extend his business before choosing a moment to retire (Luke 12:16–21). This poor woman, in sharp contrast, was willing to part with what little wealth she had. Her happiness and fulfilment lay elsewhere.

There was no need for Jesus to drive home the lesson. He had said it to them often enough: 'Blessed are you who are poor' (Luke 6:20). Why? Because they did not have the distractions of wealth or the temptations of power. The poor were dependent, and that was the first lesson of faith. This lesson might stand on its head all that they had been taught about God blessing the righteous with prosperity, but it was a key principle of the kingdom. 'Blessed' (*makarios* in Greek) literally means 'happy'. The poor, Jesus said on another occasion, were happy because 'theirs is the kingdom of heaven' (Matthew 5:3). Not only that, but the poor can be generous in a way that the rich can't. The rich can only give out of abundance. The poor give all that they have.

A reflection

The rich people were really poor; the poor widow was truly rich. There is the paradox of the kingdom of God.

Day 25: Saturday

SIGNS AND PORTENTS

READ MARK 13:3–8.

Key verse: 'Tell us, when will this be, and what will be the sign that all these things are about to be accomplished?' (v. 4).

We saw two days ago that, as Jesus and the disciples were leaving the temple one day, its sheer size and magnificence led one of them to exclaim, 'What large stones and what large buildings!' (v. 1). Jesus' response was probably unexpected, although he had already shown in a dramatic way what he thought of the spiritual state of 'his Father's house'. 'Do you see these great buildings?' he said. 'Not one stone will be left here upon another; all will be thrown down' (v. 2).

Jesus had said something similar on a previous occasion: 'Destroy this temple, and in three days I will raise it up' (John 2:19). Words like these were used as ammunition by the prosecution in the trial of Jesus, where it was alleged that Jesus had said, 'I will destroy this temple that is made with hands, and in three days I will build another, not made with hands' (Mark 14:58). Although the words used here have an authentic ring about them—that's to say, they sound like Jesus—they are not recorded as his in any of the Gospels. John explains the words about 'raising up in three days' as a reference to Jesus' resurrection (John 2:21).

In any case, Jesus was quite explicit in his contempt for the temple authorities. He clearly believed and taught that the religious system they represented was to be replaced by a new regime, inaugurated by himself as Messiah, which would be based on the principle of the kingdom of God, not human hierarchies. Its worship would centre on a temple 'not made with hands' (as his accusers put it), a spiritual house in which spiritual sacrifices would be offered. This new order could come in only if the old order was abolished, and today's reading is the beginning of a series of prophetic statements by Jesus about the events that would bring that about.

It's obvious that this chapter in Mark, and parallel ones in Matthew (slightly extended: chapter 24) and Luke (much shorter: 17:22–37), bring together warnings, pictures and prophecies relating to at least two and possibly three distinct future events— perhaps spoken at different times but gathered together in one discourse by the Gospel writers. This can lead to confusion for the reader. Some of the prophecies woul be fulfilled quite soon, within the lifetime of Jesus' hearers, it would seem. Others are obviously to be placed much further in the future, at a time known only to the Father (Mark 13:32).

The accuracy of these prophecies has led some biblical scholars to date the Gospels well after AD70 (implying that the writers were simply putting known events into prophetic language). However, it is not a historical fact that 'one stone [of the temple] will not be left here upon another; all will be thrown down', and that would certainly have been widely known after the event. There were considerable built remains, which were later adapted by various occupants of the site. This suggests that Mark and Matthew, at least, were recording a genuine prophetic statement made by Jesus before the event, which fits in with the probable dating of the Gospels.

The first series of events of which Jesus speaks concerns the immediate fate of the Jewish people, described in terms of horrific suffering (vv. 14–23), with 'desolating sacrilege set up where it ought not to be' (in the place of the temple?) and the residents of Judea fleeing to the mountains for refuge. False messiahs would arise, offering spurious remedies for the plight of the desperate people, who would suffer in a way never seen before (v. 19). There can be little doubt that this refers to the appalling events following the Jewish uprising against the Romans, which began in AD66 (just after the temple's completion), brought massive retaliation by the Roman legions and ended with destruction in AD70. When it was over, the great temple of Herod lay in ruins and the Jewish people were dispersed, some into the rural areas and mountains and others across the Middle East. It was, indeed, the end of the old order. Without a temple there could be no sacrifices; without sacrifices there could be no priesthood; without the priesthood the old hierarchy of their religion was effectively abolished. Judaism became, as it has remained, a synagogue-based religion, without priests and without sacrifices for sin. The old temple order had indeed, as Jesus foretold, been destroyed, but a new order was to rise from its ashes.

Today's reading is a kind of prologue to this prophetic discourse. The four 'core' apostles—Peter, James, John and Andrew—asked Jesus 'privately' (v. 3) when these events (the tearing down of the temple) would occur and what would be the sign that they were imminent. Jesus' immediate reply seemed a strange one: the sign would be that things would continue much as they were. There would be false messiahs (nothing new in that), there would be wars and rumours of wars (again, nothing new), 'nation will rise against nation' (as they have always done) and earthquakes and famines would occur in 'various places' (v. 8). This sounds exactly like the world we know today, so what was Jesus saying to them?

First of all, I believe, he was saying that the appalling suffering that lay ahead was the 'birth pangs' of a new order—an order described in the next section of this chapter, in which the true Messiah gathers a new people of God and inaugurates the kingdom of God. Secondly, he was saying that they should not be alarmed by such things—not even by wars, earthquakes and famines— because a divine purpose was, in some mysterious way, being worked out through it all.

This is not a palatable message for us to hear or read because we don't welcome terrible events and often find it very hard to see in human suffering (including, perhaps, our own) the marks of God's purpose. There is no suggestion, of course, that God *sends* the wars, conflicts, earthquakes and famines. In one sense, they are either part of the way the world is or they are consequences of human sin and rebellion against God. As Creator, however, he is able to use these events as building blocks of better things, as ways of bringing about a new order, perhaps, or teaching us important lessons about our own nature and the perils of living life as though God did not exist. The troubles, as Jesus daringly put it, are 'birth pangs' (v. 8)—real pain that leads to new life.

A reflection

Jesus paints a stark picture here, but we would have to admit that it is an accurate reflection of the kind of world we live in. Our would-be 'messiahs' are sometimes purveyors of false religious delusions but more often the propagandists of political or other secular ideologies. Wars and conflicts continue. Earthquakes and famines still devastate parts of our planet, causing untold misery and suffering. Yet, while that is happening, the good news of the kingdom will be preached throughout the world 'as a testimony to all the nations' (Matthew 24:14). If only the nations would listen!

Day 26: Sunday

FOLLOWING THE LIGHT

READ JOHN 8:12.

'I am the light of the world. Whoever follows me will never walk in darkness but will have the light of life.'

Most people living in the Western world today have no idea what real darkness is like. I grew up in a tiny village perched on the side of a mountain in central Wales. At night there were no street lights—in fact, no electricity, just the glimmer of oil lamps through cottage windows and, on a clear night, moon and stars. On a cloudy night, 20 yards from our house there was near-total darkness.

Many years later, used to living in the constant artificial light of a London suburb, we visited the Dan yr Ogof caves near Neath. We walked through the long and echoing chambers, illuminated by lamps, until we reached the vast central cavern, at which point our guide dramatically switched off the lights. There were muted screams of horror from the visitors. It was not simply dark: there was an almost oppressive blackness that seemed to hold us in its grip, a feeling of pressure on our open but unseeing eyes. This was real darkness! It was a huge relief when, a few seconds later, the guide switched the lights back on.

That incident comes to mind whenever I read in John's Gospel of Christ as the light—the 'light of the world', the 'true light which enlightens everyone', the light that 'shines in the darkness and the darkness did not overcome it' (1:5, 9). The ancient world knew about darkness and its perils. After nightfall, which comes early and at almost the same time throughout the year in the Middle East, the lamps were lit and a meal might be eaten. It was then time for bed, because nothing useful could happen in the darkness. The fields could not be tilled; the harvest could not be gathered; journeys could not be undertaken. Worse still, darkness was cover for thieves and brigands, for sheep stealers and assassins. Honest people stayed indoors. It is, in the words of Jesus, 'all who do evil' who hate the light (3:20).

All through John's Gospel the motif runs: Christ is the light; he brings light; he sheds light. Those who love light come to him; those who prefer darkness turn away from him. Those who follow him walk in the 'light of life' (the life-giving light), instead of stumbling along in the dark. To follow Jesus is to follow the one with the light and, on a journey that necessarily takes us through dark places, that is a very reassuring thought.

A reflection

Most of us, at some time or another in life, have felt as though we were stumbling along in the dark. For those who follow Christ, that should never be more than a fleeting experience, because his light is shining on our path. Perhaps it is our eyes that are shut to the light, rather than that the light has gone out.

Day 27: Monday

THE OPPOSITION

READ MARK 13:9–13.

Key verse: 'The one who endures to the end will be saved' (v. 13).

It's hard to imagine what the disciples would have made of this discourse. By now they would have been well aware that following Jesus was not simply a sublime short cut to power and glory. Indeed, grouped there in the courts of the temple, they would have seen afresh the reality of his and their situation. Palm Sunday was already a fast-fading memory of an hour or two of excitement; now they stood on the threshold of darkness, if they were to believe all that Jesus had been telling them. These mighty walls and, outside them, the blatant symbols of the power of imperial Rome, were reminders of what it could mean to fall into the hands of wicked men. Wars and rumours of wars, all the signs and portents of the coming kingdom, were less immediately relevant to them than their own fate—which Jesus now began to describe: 'As for yourselves…' (v. 9). At those words he must have been guaranteed their total concentration. 'Yes, Master—what about us?'

What followed would probably not have reassured them. They would face opposition from both Jewish authorities ('councils' is literally 'Sanhedrins', the religious body that advised the high priests) and Gentile ones—'kings and governors'. In fact, the crucifixion of Jesus could be seen as the work of an evil coalition of the willing, as the interests of the Roman governor, Pilate and the temple authorities came together in a desire to be rid of this troublesome prophet, Jesus.

That combination of opposition would continue long after the events of Good Friday and the resurrection. Over the first three centuries of its history, the emerging Church of Christ faced opposition from both the Jewish leadership, who condemned the movement as a dangerous and evil blasphemy, and the Roman authorities, who saw it as a direct challenge to the divine role of the emperor. Eventually the Jewish opposition faded, largely as a result of the dispersion of the Jewish people after the events of AD70, but not before angry and cruel accusations had been hurled across the divide from both sides, thus distorting Jewish–Christian relationships until modern times.

As the Jewish opposition faded or became less of a threat, however, the Church faced another and more powerful opposition. It was subjected to wave after wave of the most vicious persecution by the Roman authorities. Sometimes this was local, based on the whim of a regional governor; sometimes it was imperial, Christians being hunted down, arrested and killed all over the vast length of the Roman empire, often for refusing to burn incense before statues of the emperor. Estimates of the probable extent of the slaughter are hard to come by, but conservatively the number of executions would run to hundreds of thousands, and some would place it higher. The Romans did not see this persecution as religious in motivation. For them, the Christians were subversive of the state, disloyal citizens and a disruptive and even revolutionary element in public life.

All this would have sounded like grim news to the listening disciples. Was there a silver lining to these storm clouds brewing ahead? Yes, there was, but they might not have seen it that way. Their stand for Christ—indeed, their martyrdom—would be a 'testimony' to unbelievers (v. 9). Under accusation, the Holy Spirit would give them the words to speak, and their courage and suffering would be the most eloquent apologetic for the gospel. As the Christian philosopher Tertullian (160–225) put it, 'The blood of the martyrs was the seed of the Church'. No period in church history has seen more rapid growth or so many die for the faith.

In fact, the Greek word for 'martyr' simply means 'witness'. The two things were synonymous in those early centuries of Christianity. To confess faith in Jesus was to risk death, but to face death for the sake of belief in the resurrection was the most convincing proof of its reality. After all, among the martyrs were, very probably, ten of the original twelve apostles, together with Paul, the great if 'untimely born' apostle to the Gentiles (1 Corinthians 15:8). They died with the claim on their lips that they had seen the risen Jesus. It's hard to think of a more compelling argument for the truth of that claim.

So the first reward for faithfulness under the coming persecution would be the knowledge that it would be a 'testimony', not just to the Jewish people but to 'all nations' (Mark 13:10).

The second reward ends this particular part of the discourse. Although they would be universally hated because of confessing Christ (even within their own families, perhaps), 'the one who endures to the end will be saved' (v. 13). Endurance is not a Christian virtue much talked about in today's Western Church. We prefer to think of the benefits of faith—love, joy, peace, forgiveness, contentment and so on. Yet, over the history of the Church, endurance has been a notable mark of the real thing. Paul, James and Peter, in their New Testament letters, all speak of it as the ultimate test of faith, without which faith is revealed as inadequate and shallow (see, for example, Romans 5:3; Titus 2:2; James 1:3; 2 Peter 1:6). To 'endure' is to overcome what is hard and tough, to suffer patiently, and such would be the lot of these first Christian witnesses. Yet out of their endurance would come salvation: the one who endures to the end will be saved—brought to wholeness and completeness in Christ.

Before the end comes (the end of the time of trial and the end of the age), 'the good news must first be proclaimed to all nations' (Mark 13:10). The witness of the martyrs and the message of Jesus and the resurrection will continue during the dark days and will finally usher in the lifting of the clouds and the glorious Day of the Lord—but that vision constitutes the final section of this temple discourse.

A reflection

'Do not worry beforehand about what you are to say' is not advice for preachers who might be tempted not to bother preparing a sermon! Instead, it is a promise to Christians under pressure—perhaps those the apostle Peter speaks about who are required to give 'an account of the hope that is in you'—that they will be given words with which to answer their questioners (1 Peter 3:15).

Day 28: Tuesday

BEING PREPARED

READ MARK 13:32–37.

Key verse: 'Beware, keep alert; for you do not know when the time will come' (v. 33).

Jesus offered his listening disciples certain signs and portents of the coming events, particularly of the point at which the new order, under the Messiah Jesus, would be ushered in. When the fig tree produces leaves, you know that summer is near (v. 28). So, when the awful events Jesus had described to them occur, they may equally well know that the winter of suffering and struggle is coming to an end. The prophet from Galilee will take his appointed place as Lord of the Church and the inaugurator of the kingdom of God. This will not be the end of time but it will be the end of an age. The old order of religion will have given way to the new. Law, in its narrow sense, will have given way to grace. Access to God will not be through priests, sacrifices and rituals, but through the Messiah Jesus. Nothing will be the same again.

Now, however, in today's reading, he invites them to look further into the future. The events he had already spoken of would occur before the last member of 'this generation' (v. 30) had died: the uprising and the dispersal of the Jewish people happened less than 40 years after these words were spoken by Jesus. But there is another, even more important event which lies in a future beyond that, something that will occur at a day and hour no one knows, 'neither the angels in heaven, nor the Son, but only the Father'

(v. 32). That is the date of the return of Christ, which we call the second coming.

If even Jesus on earth did not know the date, it does seem a bit presumptuous, to say the least, of mere human beings (even if they are eloquent preachers or deeply versed in the scriptures) to claim that they do know. The Church has lived since the resurrection in a permanent state of waiting, not knowing when this final triumphant event will take place. The early Church clearly thought that it was imminent—indeed, some were impatient for its arrival (see 2 Peter 3:4). Yet the apostles constantly emphasized the teaching of Jesus that the 'Day of the Lord' would come 'like a thief in the night', unannounced and unheralded (1 Thessalonians 5:2).

The word that the New Testament uses for this coming is *parousia*, which actually means 'appearing'. In some way, almost certainly not one that we could predict or expect, the Saviour of the world will 'appear'—be seen and recognized. There is a brilliant poem by a modern poet, John Burnside, called simply 'Parousia'. In it he suggests a different, less dramatic interpretation of that final 'appearing' of Jesus:

> *I think, if it came, there would be*
> *something more subtle:*
> *a blur at the corner of vision, a trick of the light,*
> *or the notion that things have shifted*
> *closer...*

This contrasts, it must be said, with the language the New Testament uses about the second coming, which generally has a triumphalist ring to it ('power and great glory... the clouds of heaven', and so on). However, there were prophecies of the first coming of Christ, yet when it happened no one recognized it for what it was unless they were specifically told. It took them all—biblical scholars, magi, kings and shepherds—totally by surprise. They had expected a kingly birth, presumably in a palace. What they got was a baby lying in a feeding trough in some overflow accommodation in Bethlehem. It's always dangerous to second-guess God!

This theme of the *parousia* taking people by surprise is expanded in Matthew's account of the discourse. It will be like the flood in the days of Noah, which took everyone by surprise except for his household (Matthew 24:37). It will be like a thief coming in the dead of night, unannounced and unexpected, to break into someone's house (v. 43). This secret coming will divide colleagues and friends—'one will be taken and one will be left' (vv. 40–41), with no clear indication which of those is the better fate, it must be said.

The only way to cope with the *parousia*, with this mysterious 'appearing' of Jesus, will be readiness: be ready, be alert, keep your guard, don't fall asleep spiritually. That has been the constant burden of the Church's teaching about the second coming. We don't know, and aren't intended to know, when it will be, but we have the word of Christ that it will happen and that it will be marvellous for his people, the people of the kingdom. They need to be constantly ready for it, living their lives as though, at any moment, the Son of Man might come—in whatever guise or circumstances.

A reflection

Jesus said to his disciples, 'What I say to you I say to all: Keep awake' (Mark 13:37). He also said, 'Be on guard so that your hearts are not weighed down with dissipation and drunkenness and the worries of this life, and that day does not catch you unexpectedly, like a trap... Be alert at all times' (Luke 21:34–36).

THE CONSPIRACY

READ MATTHEW 26:1–5, 14–16

*Key verses: Then the chief priests and the elders of the people
gathered in the palace of the high priest, who was called
Caiaphas, and they conspired to arrest Jesus by stealth and kill
him (vv. 3–4).*

It was now only two days to Passover and the disciples might just
have been thinking that things had been going quite well in
Jerusalem. Jesus had arrived with a noisy reception committee, it
was true, and had then caused a minor furore in the temple courts
by overturning the stalls of the money changers. Yet, for all his talk
about impending doom, on the whole he had been well received
by the crowds and he had dealt more than satisfactorily (and, on
the whole, quite gently) with various cross-examinations by the
Sadducees and Pharisees (see, for example, Matthew 22:15–45).
Indeed, those debates ended with a peremptory footnote from
Matthew: 'nor from that day did anyone dare to ask him any more
questions' (v. 46).

If the disciples had deduced from that signs of a softening of the
authorities' attitude to Jesus or of his powerful condemnation of
them, they were to be proved sadly wrong. In the first place, he told
them himself that all his direst words about his future destiny were
about to be fulfilled. 'You know that after two days the Passover is
coming, and the Son of Man will be handed over to be crucified'
(26:2). This is stark indeed. There is no mention here (as the

Gospel writers had been careful to record previously) of a resurrection on the third day. His words are short on detail—no 'hands of wicked men', no mention of betrayal or beatings—but powerful in their simplicity. In two days' time, it will happen. He will be 'handed over' (an interesting wording) and crucified. The words of Jesus would have struck home with chilling effect, given the temple location and the proximity of the Passover. Until now, they had been able to put his warnings into the category of 'one day'—a bit like global warming for people today. But 'two days' would have concentrated their minds powerfully.

While Jesus was speaking, the chief priests and elders were having a meeting in the high priest's palace. The subject of their discussion was the prophet from Galilee, Jesus of Nazareth. It may be that their deliberations were made all the more urgent by his recent debating victories over the Sadducees and Pharisees. Jumped-up revolutionaries and miracle-working messiahs they could deal with, but to be made to look ridiculous over matters of biblical interpretation by a carpenter's son from the backwoods was intolerable.

There were also, of course, other words of Jesus to take into account. In recent days he had abandoned any semblance of guarded language about the future of the Jewish nation in its present form—and certainly under its present leadership. Nothing could have been clearer or more devastating than his story of the landowner and the vineyard (Matthew 21:33–41). He told this parable to an audience in the temple courts that included those same 'chief priests and the elders of the people' (v. 23). None of his listeners could have been in the slightest doubt about the identity of the main characters in the story or of the 'vineyard' where it took place. After all, Israel is constantly called God's 'vine' by the Hebrew prophets or, even more specifically, his 'pleasant vineyard' (Isaiah 27:2), intended to fill the world with its fruit.

Yet in this story the landowner, presumably the Lord, is appalled to find that the tenants of his vineyard, the people of Israel, are treating its produce as their own and refusing to yield to him what is rightfully due. Worse than that, they reject his servants (the prophets?), beating up some and killing others. Finally he sends his son, assuming that they will respect him, yet they kill him and seize the vineyard for themselves. The response of the landowner is immediate: he will judge the 'wretches' (v. 41) who did this and lease the vineyard to other tenants (presumably the despised Gentiles).

The message could not have been clearer. In rejecting Jesus, they were rejecting the Messiah and Son of God, and the consequences would be terrible beyond words. In the light of all this, it's not surprising that the Gospels record a conspiracy to arrest Jesus by stealth—though not, apparently, during Passover, when the city was full of Jews from other provinces, including many Galileans. The arrest of so charismatic a preacher under those conditions might well have given rise to rioting.

The high priest who presided over the meeting was Caiaphas, the son-in-law of Annas, who had been high priest before him but, according to John's Gospel, still seems to have had considerable influence. Caiaphas held office from AD18 to 37. The power that these religious leaders held was entirely at the mercy of the Roman authorities—indeed, high priests were directly appointed by the Prefect, Pontius Pilate, so they were constantly aware that dismissal might follow if anything they did caused him embarrassment or worse. Equally, Pilate was constantly aware that he was under close scrutiny from Rome for past failures. In fact, he was finally recalled by the emperor in AD37 for cruel repression in Samaria. So there was a coalition of mutual interest between him and the temple leaders.

All of this meant that the Jewish authorities had to work clandestinely up to the point at which they had Jesus under detention and could present him to Pilate as a troublemaker and creator of dissension. If that object was to be achieved, they would need to arrest him in circumstances where there was no crowd present—preferably after dark and in a private location. They probably knew that Jesus and his disciples spent their nights at Bethany, but would prefer a location for his arrest that was even more private. It seems they let it be known that they would welcome information as to the future whereabouts of Jesus.

This brings Judas Iscariot into the scene. Until now, all that the Gospels have given us are dark hints; even when the names of the Twelve are recorded, the list ends '... and Judas Iscariot, the one who betrayed him' (see, for instance, Matthew 10:4). We shall be examining his role in more detail later, but at this stage we can note that he took the initiative in going to the chief priests, having presumably heard in some way that they were seeking to arrest Jesus by stealth. They struck a deal with him and 'from that moment he began to look for an opportunity to betray Jesus' (26:16).

The other disciples would have been completely unaware of all this, but it became obvious that Jesus knew very well what was going on, including the involvement of one of his followers. This may have contributed to a change in his demeanour: John calls it being 'troubled in soul' (12:27). The disciples, who were accustomed to look to him for constant encouragement and support, may have felt that even their leader and teacher was subject to the anxieties and fears that were besetting them. We can detect in the Gospel narratives a distinct edginess among them, a feeling of anxious foreboding. It was to last for no more than another five days—had they but known it.

A reflection

Sometimes anxieties seem to overwhelm faith, but in the case of Jesus they actually seemed to strengthen it. His soul was 'troubled' at the prospect of what lay ahead, yet he could say, 'It is for this reason that I have come to this hour' (John 12:27). In other words, the purpose of his heavenly Father would make what lay ahead worthwhile. Human beings are all subject to anxiety, but we are also creatures of hope. For the Christian, the two are always linked because we can know, as Jesus did, that it is the 'God of hope' (Romans 15:13) who marks out our path, even when we can't see the way.

THE TRAGEDY
OF JERUSALEM

READ MATTHEW 23:37–39; LUKE 19:42.

Key verse: 'If you, even you, had only recognized on this day the things that make for peace!' (Luke 19:42).

About a thousand years before Jesus and his disciples walked the temple courts, Jerusalem was founded by King David. He acquired the site by conquest, recognizing that it held a strategically neutral position almost on the border between Israel (the ten tribes) and Judah (the other two). It was, in fact, just inside the territory of the tribe of Judah, but at its northern extremity. By making Jerusalem his capital and seat of government, David hoped to unite the twelve tribes, the descendants of Jacob. By selecting a site (on Mount Moriah) for a temple, David also hoped to make Jerusalem the religious centre of the Jewish people. The temple was duly built by his son Solomon and for nearly a thousand years the site was the spiritual heart of the nation.

Sadly, invasions, conquests and incursions meant that the temple needed to be rebuilt several times, and not until the time of Jesus did it bear any comparison with the glory of the temple built by Solomon. When Herod the Great was installed in 37BC with the support of the Romans, who had by then occupied the land in place of the previous Greek conquerors, he set about building the vast edifice that had left the disciples so awestruck. It occupied almost a quarter of the total area of the city. Herod's vision was not shared by all the Jews, however. The stricter ones were uneasy about his mixed race—Jewish and Idumaean.

Jerusalem's importance for the Jewish people depended on much more than bricks and stones. Not only was it the centre of their worship and the place of religious sacrifice, but its very name was identified with national aspirations. The psalmist sang of its glories and gave the city an almost mystic significance. It symbolized the ideals and hope of the Jewish people and led to the concept of a future 'new Jerusalem', where God would reign as king over all the earth and 'Jerusalem shall abide in security' (see Zechariah 14:8–11).

For all those reasons, the disciples and the crowds who were listening to Jesus in the temple courts would have been both shocked and saddened by what he had to say about the city. His words came at the end of a blistering attack on hypocritical religion, especially as exemplified by many of the Pharisees and teachers of the law. He described them as 'whitewashed tombs' (Matthew 23:27), beautiful in appearance but full of death inside. He likened them to all the evil men who had persecuted and murdered God's faithful prophets in the past. Now the day of judgment had come.

At that point Jesus broke into a lament for the city: 'Jerusalem, Jerusalem, the city that kills the prophets and stones those who are sent to it!' (v. 37). That was the tragedy of past failure, but the heart of Jesus was broken for the city as it lay there around him: 'How often have I desired to gather your children together as a hen gathers her brood under her wings, and you were not willing!' The tragedy of Jerusalem was of opportunity spurned, not only in the past but now, at this moment, as its people failed to recognize and receive their Messiah. The price would be terrible indeed—a 'desolate house' (v. 38) inhabited by people who would not see the one who could have brought them blessing until the day of his triumphal return.

Luke dramatically places these sayings about Jerusalem earlier, on the day of the triumphal entry. It's not at all unlikely, of course, that Jesus expressed similar sentiments several times during these last days in the city. On this occasion, riding on the ass through crowds of cheering disciples, 'as he came near and saw the city, he wept over it' (Luke 19:41). He saw its towers, domes, palaces and the great temple before him, but he also saw with dreadful prophetic clarity a day not far in the future when enemies would besiege the city and crush all of it to the ground, not leaving 'one stone upon another' (vv. 43–44).

Jesus also gave a reason for this tragedy—a failure to recognize the significance of what was happening among them: 'If you, even you, had only recognized on this day the things that make for peace!' (v. 42). It was the good news of the kingdom that made for peace. It was the vision Jesus brought of a people who would love their enemies, go the second mile, turn the other cheek and love God and neighbour with all their hearts that made for peace. But they had rejected it, either by deliberate decision or by neglect, and now it would be 'hidden from their eyes'. Unlike blind Bartimaeus, they had missed the moment of divine opportunity and what followed would be inevitable. No wonder Jesus wept.

Nearly 40 years later the tension between the Jews and their Roman conquerors burst into open rebellion. The uprising was doomed from the start. Once again the city of God was destroyed, as Jesus had warned it would be if its inhabitants neglected the way of peace. A temple to Jupiter was erected on the temple site, fulfilling the words of Jesus about 'the desolating sacrilege set up where it ought not to be' (Mark 13:14). Jews were banished from their own city, which became for 200 years a Roman garrison town until Constantine established it as a Christian city in the fourth century. Even now, 2000 years later, Jerusalem is the hub of the world's most intransigent conflict, this time between Jews and Muslims, whose claim to the city is based on the belief that Mohammed was taken up into heaven from the site of the self-same temple.

David's original vision of Jerusalem as a place of religious and political unity lasted only a century or two, as the northern tribes split from the south and various pagan cults also infiltrated the city's outskirts. The hope now rests in those stern words of Jesus to the people of the city in his day: 'You will not see me again until you say, "Blessed is the one who comes in the name of the Lord"' (Matthew 23:39). At least one day, it seems, they will be joining in the welcoming cries of the disciples on the Mount of Olives as they too greet the Lord Messiah.

A reflection

The kingdom values that Jesus taught are still the 'things that make for peace'. They include a care for the marginalized, poor and oppressed, a longing for justice and peace, an openness to human suffering and need and the grace to love those from whom we differ, even when we differ profoundly. Such things can still be overlooked or ignored, however, even by those who profess to follow Christ.

Day 31: Friday

THE UPPER ROOM

READ LUKE 22:7–13.

Key verse: Then came the day of Unleavened Bread, on which the Passover lamb had to be sacrificed (v. 7).

They probably didn't have notices up in the markets in Jerusalem saying, 'Only three shopping days to Passover', but the air of expectancy was certainly there. Normally the city's population at that time was about 25,000, but at Passover it trebled, with visitors and pilgrims from across the Mediterranean lands heading for the ancient centre of Jewish worship to celebrate the feast together.

Some years ago, I was privileged to share the Passover meal in Jerusalem with a Jewish family and realized in a fresh way what a variety of needs and experiences it brought together. Passover is a family occasion, rather like Christmas; but it is also a national and religious one, combining something of the festival of a patron saint (David or Andrew, for instance) with a solemn remembrance of a great salvation in the past and the hope of a coming Messiah in the future. It is about Israel, of course, but it is also about Israel's dependence on the God who brought them from slavery and set them in their own land. It identifies the Jewish people as the people whom God redeemed and led through the wilderness and so gives them both a history and a future.

The disciples, most of them Galileans unused to the bustle of the city, would have been caught up in the excitement and expectation of the festival, especially as Jesus involved them in the preparations for the *seder*, the Passover meal. According to Luke, these preparations took place on the day when 'the Passover lamb had to be sacrificed' (v. 7). It's hard to reconstruct in any detail the way in which the Passover was celebrated at the time of Jesus because, over the centuries, many little things had been added to the ritual and some had been omitted. It would seem that at this period the lambs for the Passover were collectively sacrificed, presumably in the temple, rather than being slaughtered at home, as they would have been on the night before the exodus.

Although Jewish people no longer sacrifice a lamb in this ritual sense, the heart of the *seder* meal still is, as it always was, the eating of roast meat—the lamb—and of unleavened bread, and the passing round of a cup of wine at several points in the meal. These actions recalled the last meal of the Israelites before they left Egypt in haste, but they were complemented by the retelling of the story of the exodus. So, in word and action, they made a permanent remembrance of the great event that brought into being a new nation, Israel, and a new religion, Judaism; and in doing so they renewed their covenant relationship with the Lord God of their fathers.

Jesus told his disciples precisely how they were to make preparations for their celebration—not as a family in the biological sense but as the nucleus of the new covenant family of God. Peter and John were sent off to the city to book the room where they would share the meal together. When they had entered the city, they would see a man carrying a jar of water. This unusual sight would identify him as a resident of the house in which it was to take place.

Carrying jars of water (usually on the head) was definitely female work, so a man doing it would probably have been an object of ridicule or, at least, considerable attention. It has been suggested that the only men in Jerusalem to carry their own water jars would have been the members of the monastic Qumran community by the Dead Sea. If the man in question was indeed an Essene, that would suggest a degree of fraternization between Jesus and these Jewish zealots (the makers and keepers of the Dead Sea Scrolls), which would be surprising but not impossible. It might also help to explain a certain perceived contradiction in the Gospel accounts about the precise days and times of the Passover festival that year. The Essenes, wishing to have nothing to do with the corrupt temple and its leaders, observed the feast on a different day.

Be that as it may, the disciples could hardly miss a jar-carrying male and consequently followed him to his house, where they would be introduced to its owner. He would show them a large upstairs room, already 'furnished' (v. 12)—that is, presumably, ready for the *seder* meal. They were to confirm the booking, as it were, and then prepare the meal itself.

The upper room has, of course, entered into the collective memory of Christian spirituality. 'The night he was betrayed' is synonymous in our thinking with this particular place, and this particular name for it. Yet there was nothing innately spiritual about the upper room in the first century. Most houses, other than those of the really poor, were square, with a flat roof and a room downstairs where the family ate and slept—and often kept the animals, too. In addition, there was an upper room above the living space, usually reached by outside stairs and often used for social or religious occasions—a visit by the rabbi for lessons or, as here, a feast of some kind or other. The nearest modern comparison might be the 'best room' that my grandmother used to keep in her little terraced house. It was seldom used, but when it was it took an important place in family life.

The Passover had been observed by the Jews of that time for over a thousand years, although there had been periods of religious apathy or apostasy when it was neglected and ignored. It was the foundational festival of the Jewish people, who were very well aware that it was through the sacrifice of a lamb 'without blemish' (Exodus 12:5) that their forefathers had been saved. Now the one who had been described by John the Baptist to Peter and John as the 'lamb of God' was about to celebrate with his disciples that same deliverance, but would also point them on to an even greater deliverance that a new sacrifice was about to win for all the people.

A reflection

'Passover' derives in English from the Hebrew word pesach, which means literally to 'pass over'. When the destroyer flew over Egypt to bring that terrible last plague on the firstborn sons of the Egyptians, it passed over the houses on whose lintels was daubed the blood of the sacrificed lamb: 'The Lord will pass through to strike down the Egyptians. When he sees the blood... the Lord will pass over that door and will not allow the destroyer to enter your houses to strike you down' (Exodus 12:23). In the moment of judgment, when the arrogance and cruelty of Pharaoh brought anguish and death to his land, there was also a moment of mercy as the slaves crouched behind their blood-daubed doors. So often, and necessarily, judgment and mercy go hand in hand.

Day 32: Saturday

THE FOOT WASHING

READ JOHN 13:1–15.

Key verse: 'If I, your Lord and Teacher, have washed your feet, you also ought to wash one another's feet' (v. 14).

It was Passover eve, the night on which Jesus was to share the *seder* with his friends. They gathered in the upper room, perhaps with an understandable degree of anxiety but also, surely, some excitement that things were clearly coming to a head. They had followed Jesus from Galilee. On the road, far up in the north, they had confessed him as the Messiah. Since then they had heard (though not, perhaps, fully comprehended) his words of warning: they were to make their way to Jerusalem, where the authorities would use force against Jesus and eventually kill him. He had often added, rather mysteriously, that on 'the third day' he would be raised. So, as they might have seen it, there was tragedy but eventually there might also be triumph. As they gathered, there would surely have been the usual banter and teasing—after all, this was a group of 20-something men—but it would be surprising if it wasn't covering a sense of excitement mingled with anxiety.

They trooped into the room, walking past a little stand on which had been placed a bowl of water and a towel. They knew what it was for, of course. It was customary for travellers stopping for a meal to have their hot, dusty feet washed in cold water—a menial task usually performed by a slave, preferably a Gentile one or a woman. There was no sign in the upper room of any slaves, or women for that matter, but presumably each disciple, as he walked past, felt that whoever else might have to fulfil this task, it couldn't possibly be him. Someone else was younger, less experienced, from a lower social group or occupation. No one wanted to take on the servant role of foot washer to the rest.

Then Jesus walked in. He looked around the room and then took the towel and wrapped it round his waist. Watched by the astonished disciples, he picked up the basin and began to wash their feet. If no one else would take on the role of a servant, then the one who later reminded them that he was their 'Lord and Teacher' (v. 13) would do it.

When he reached Peter, the embarrassment and shame of it was too much for the former fisherman. 'Lord', he asked incredulously, 'are *you* going to wash my feet?' 'You do not know now what I am doing,' said Jesus, 'but later you will understand' (vv. 6–7).

At that, Peter decided he must stop this undignified farce: 'You will never wash my feet,' he said (v. 8). The reply of Jesus was outwardly gentle, yet it concealed a serious warning: 'Unless I wash you, you have no share with me'—in other words, you are not part of my fellowship. To refuse to let Jesus wash him would be arrogance, compounding the pride that had led him to walk straight past the basin and leave the job to someone inferior. Peter took the point instantly and, being the kind of man he was, decided that if washing was part of belonging to Jesus he would go for the full bath: 'Lord, not my feet only, but also my hands and my head' (v. 9)—not just my feet that stray but my hands that touch forbidden things and my head that brings me temptation.

There was no need for so drastic a baptism, was the reply of Jesus. You (all of you) have been 'bathed' (v. 10), made clean, by becoming my disciples. Someone who has had a bath doesn't need to go and bathe again just because they encounter the occasional soiling of the day. Just the feet will do, to remove the grime and dirt of the journey.

So it is on the journey of faith. Every time we fail we do not need to be 'baptized' all over again. We have been made clean by the grace of God. Yet on that journey we all pick up, from time to time, the specks and stains of failure, of our own sin and disobedience. The answer is the 'foot-washing'—the removal of the consequences of the day's minor defeats and setbacks, the sins and failures that will accompany us right to the end of our earthly journey of faith. The same Lord whose cross and passion set us on the road is the one who now will maintain us on the journey. The day's failures can be forgiven, preferably before the next day begins. Then the slate is clean, the account has been paid in full by the Saviour and we can resume our pilgrimage unencumbered.

When the washing was done, Jesus took the opportunity to drive home its lesson. He took off the towel and replaced the basin before taking his seat at the table. He affirmed that he was indeed their 'Lord' and 'Rabbi', deserving of respect, but, he insisted, 'If I, your Lord and Teacher, have washed your feet, you also ought to wash one another's feet' (v. 14). What he had done, he explained, was to give them an example. He had washed their feet, literally. They should from now on 'wash one another's feet'—that is, take the place of humility, accept the role of the servant and, as servants, both of Christ and of his people, learn to serve. In this way, and only in this way, they would mirror the ministry of Jesus and be able faithfully to proclaim his message.

His words undoubtedly went home. We can see them ringingly endorsed in Paul's second letter to the Corinthians, speaking of the ministry of the apostles: 'We do not proclaim ourselves; we proclaim Jesus Christ as Lord and ourselves as your slaves for Jesus' sake' (4:5). As this memorable evening wore on and as the little band moved off to the garden of Gethsemane and all the dark events that followed it, they would have reason to remember the words of Jesus. Neither he nor they were called to worldly power, respect or honour. That was not the way of the cross.

A reflection

The Christian Church, both in its universal sense and locally, has been hideously distorted time and again, throughout its history, by issues of status and hierarchy. Many of the petty disputes that tear our congregations apart are nominally about doctrinal issues but in fact about power and personality. The Church of Jesus Christ exists to continue his own ministry of self-sacrificial love and service, not to provide a platform for power politics or the cult of personality. It was a message that Jesus had emphasized to his disciples time after time, but it needed this powerful and shocking visual aid finally to drive the message home. Those who, in any way, think of Christian ministry in terms of power or status have simply got it all wrong.

Day 33: Sunday

THE SECRET FOLLOWERS

READ JOHN 12:36–37, 42–43.

Key verse: They loved human glory more than the glory that comes from God (v. 43).

In some ways these are among the most revealing and saddest verses in the Gospels. They tell us that even the authorities, presumably including the Sanhedrin, were divided over Jesus. Some, in fact, believed in him. As the final stages of the story unfold, one or two of them emerge from the shadows. The readers of John's Gospel have already met Nicodemus, who visited Jesus under cover of night to discover what he was teaching. There he is described as a Pharisee, 'a leader of the Jews' (John 3:1). Later he argued with the chief priests that Jesus should be treated justly and at least not be judged without a fair hearing (7:51). This modest stand for justice was ridiculed by his colleagues: 'Surely you are not also from Galilee, are you? Search and you will see that no prophet is to arise from Galilee' (v. 52).

Later, Nicodemus joined another dissenting voice among the ruling classes, Joseph of Arimathea, in arranging the burial of Jesus. John says of Joseph that he was 'a disciple of Jesus, though a secret one because of his fear of the Jews' (19:38)—presumably meaning, as this Gospel usually does, the Jewish rulers. After all, everybody in the story at this point is a Jew, including Jesus and the Twelve.

These secret disciples are something of a surprise. They imply that the people of Jerusalem had a rather more intimate knowledge of Jesus and his teaching than we might have gathered from the Gospels of Matthew, Mark and Luke, where his ministry is almost exclusively in Galilee and to its east and north. Of course, they speak of the Pharisees and teachers of the law coming from Jerusalem to Galilee to investigate him. Clearly there was a great deal of interest and concern in the ruling quarters about this popular teacher and healer.

Whatever conclusions individuals among the authorities reached about Jesus, however, obviously the majority view was that he posed a serious threat to the stability of the nation under Roman government and also a considerable challenge to their own power. As so often in such situations, the minority decided that their own self-preservation (and perhaps the good of the community) would be best served by silence. They were not the first or the last to adopt that strategy. There were many people in the Germany of the 1930s who secretly opposed all that Hitler and the Nazis stood for but, for rather similar reasons, decided to keep quiet. Those who didn't, like Dietrich Bonhoeffer, the Lutheran pastor, often paid a high price for their courage.

There were apparently many in this category during the last days of the life of Jesus. They believed in him, but 'because of the Pharisees… did not confess it' (12:42). John gives us a reason for that: 'for fear that they would be put out of the synagogue'—excommunicated, we might say. He also adds a typical comment of his own: 'They loved human glory more than the glory that comes from God' (v. 43).

To belong to the temple elite was to have status, prestige and a certain amount of power. The Romans were quite glad to have Jewish leadership in place, partly because it deflected resentment from them and partly because they found ruling this obstinately religious province very difficult. There had already been riots and insurrections, put down by the legions with force of arms. The Romans knew that their very presence was resented, and the signs of imperial power were regarded by many Jews as blasphemous, so it was useful at times to hide behind the Jewish religious leadership. As a reward, those leaders were given places of privilege as well as monetary and practical benefits. It may seem at a distance a pretty tawdry glory, but it has to be said that, in human history, souls have been sold for less.

The secret disciples believed in Jesus but they did not confess it, fundamentally for fear of the disapproval of their peers. Situations change, history rolls on, but still today people who believe in Jesus will not confess him publicly—and for much the same reason.

A reflection

To remain silent in the presence of injustice, cruelty or evil is, to some degree, to condone it. Speaking out is not always popular and is sometimes costly, but it is often a Christian duty. Others are entitled to know where we stand. As the apostle Paul wrote, 'If you confess with your lips that Jesus is Lord and believe in your heart that God raised him from the dead, you will be saved. For one believes with the heart and so is justified, and one confesses with the mouth and so is saved' (Romans 10:9–10). Perhaps Paul had in mind here the reluctant or secret 'disciple' and that is why he puts so much emphasis on public confession. It's a fair question to ask myself: how many people know that I am a Christian?

JUDAS, THE BETRAYER

READ JOHN 13:21–30.

Key verse: Jesus answered, 'It is the one to whom I give this piece of bread when I have dipped it in the dish.' So when he had dipped the piece of bread, he gave it to Judas son of Simon Iscariot (v. 26).

At the meal in the upper room, as John describes it, Jesus was acting as host at the table. On his right reclined John. Possibly on his immediate left, or perhaps further around the table, was Judas Iscariot, who acted as treasurer for the group. John was a former fisherman and, like ten of the others, he was a Galilean. Judas, his name suggests, came from Karioth, which would mean that he was the only one of the Twelve who was a Judean. That in itself served to separate him from the others in terms of culture, background and dialect. It may also have given him an inbuilt sense of superiority, Galileans being generally regarded as rather rustic and unsophisticated by the residents of the southern region, with Jerusalem as its cultural and spiritual centre.

Along with the other eleven, Judas had been chosen by Jesus after a night of prayer in the hills. They were in one sense a motley band, including a Zealot (freedom fighter, presumably reformed), several fishermen from Lake Galilee, a former tax collector, and two who bore the name Judas—one simply described as 'son of James' and the other, always bringing up the rear of the list, Judas Iscariot. Matthew and Mark simply describe Judas Iscariot as the one 'who betrayed him'. Luke, perhaps more perceptively, says that he *became* a traitor' (Luke 6:16). That leaves open the possibility that, when chosen by Jesus, he met the requirements of a future apostle but that something happened between then and the end of the journey which caused him to become what he wasn't before (and perhaps wasn't by nature): a traitor.

On the evening of the *seder*, Judas' position among the disciples (also called apostles) was confirmed by a place at the table. He was one of the family, even if not occupying quite as intimate a place as that given to John, 'the one whom Jesus loved' (John 13:23). It would be wrong to think of Jesus as having favourites. Like most of us, Jesus could love and be committed to the whole group while still regarding one or two of them as his particular confidantes. On this occasion, John is clearly in that position because, when Jesus caused consternation by stating in the most emphatic way ('very truly') that 'one of you will betray me' (v. 21), Peter gestured to John to ask Jesus to identify the traitor. So, while reclining next to him, the 'beloved disciple' took the opportunity to ask, 'Lord, who is it?' (v. 25).

Jesus' answer appeared enigmatic: 'It is the one to whom I give this piece of bread when I have dipped it in the dish' (v. 26). In the event, it was immediately clear whom he meant because he took the bread, dipped it and handed it to Judas. It is said that this was a courtesy of the time—to give to the most honoured guest the first piece of bread. If so (and it sounds reasonable), Jesus was saying to Judas, 'You are still my friend, still my disciple, still loved and honoured by me. The choice is yours. You can identify with me and respond to my love or you can go ahead with what I know you are thinking of doing.' It seems that Jesus was giving Judas a last chance to pull back from the course of action on which he had set himself. Whatever Judas did, Jesus wished him to know that the choice was entirely his own. He was loved and valued by Jesus, and he must know that.

In fact, Judas took the bread and ate it but without any repentance, without any change of purpose. John describes the moment with chilling insight: 'After he received the bread, Satan entered into him' (v. 27). In that moment, as it were, the potential friend and apostle of Jesus became his adversary, which is the literal meaning of 'satan'.

The decision having been made, there was no turning back. Jesus spoke quietly to Judas: 'Do quickly what you are going to do.' No one else around the table was aware of all this, but Judas heard the words, got up from the table and left the room. As he opened the door to leave, John must have noticed that darkness had set in since they arrived at the house. 'And it was night,' he records (v. 30).

Judas the betrayer was to become a hated figure in early Christian thought. He was depicted as the apotheosis of evil, the man who handed over the world's Saviour to his enemies. In medieval art he is often portrayed as inhabiting the darkest and vilest spot in hell. The 30 pieces of silver that he was paid for the deed have also entered into human mythology as symbols of greed or as representing the price that a traitor might demand for his treachery.

For the serious reader of the Gospels, this is too simplistic. The questions persist. How could, or why did, Jesus choose a disciple who was so prone to the common temptation of greed? Why should a man who had heard the teaching of Jesus, seen his miracles and observed his loving concern for others seem to prefer the corrupt leadership of the temple authorities or even that of the hated Romans? Was Judas predestined to damnation, as some medieval writers seemed to believe? Or was he in fact a kind of saint, a vital link in the whole process of the salvation of the human race, as the bogus 'Gospel of Judas' from the late second century seems to argue? In that case, how much real choice did Judas have?

Probably the answer is more straightforward and to be found in the complex web of politics and religion enmeshing everything that occurred in Israel, and especially Jerusalem, at that time. The longing for the coming of the Messiah and deliverance from foreign occupation was one element. The perceived corruption of the

Jewish religious leadership was another. The concept of the Messiah as 'another David', who would do what King David did and create a unified nation out of the squabbling tribes of Israel, was yet another—even though David's united kingdom had not survived for long. Many young Jewish men were caught up in this powderkeg of anger, frustration and pent-up emotion. They were not prepared to sit by any longer and watch the desecration of the covenant community and the swaggering presence on its streets of Roman legionaries. Clearly Simon the Zealot had been one such man. We know nothing of Judas Iscariot until he is named among the Twelve, but it is at least possible, and even probable, that he shared those views and that his decision to follow Christ was based on the hope that he would fulfil these messianic longings. After all, if Jesus could give sight to the blind, healing to the paralysed, even life to the dead, then surely dealing with the Italian Legion was simply a matter of calling up a few squadrons of the heavenly host?

If Judas was thinking along those lines, then the developments since the transfiguration would have come as a dreadful shock to him. His vision of an Israel recreated by brave leadership and force of arms (even heavenly ones) was clearly not shared by Jesus. All this talk of going up to Jerusalem only to be handed over to wicked men and crucified must have sounded to him like sheer defeatism.

It may be (indeed, the Gospel text suggests it) that the last straw for Judas was the anointing of Jesus at Bethany. Judas would certainly have joined in the voices of those disciples who protested at the waste of the expensive ointment that was poured over the feet of Jesus, but the real shock would have been to hear him say that the woman who had done this had 'anointed his body beforehand for its burial' (Mark 14:8). It sounded as though Jesus would go meekly to his fate and that the time of his death was imminent.

The next paragraph in Mark 14 begins, '*Then* Judas Iscariot, who was one of the Twelve, went to the high priests in order to betray him to them' (v. 10). The initiative came from Judas, who did not in fact set a price for it or demand payment: 'they promised to give him money' (v. 11). His act of betrayal may have been simply frustration, the feeling that he had wasted three years of his life following yet another failed messiah. Or, as I am inclined to think, it may have been a belated attempt to force the hand of Jesus, to make him declare himself and assume that role of kingly leadership that Judas had always understood to be at the heart of messiahship.

We can never know the whole truth about Judas—at any rate, not this side of eternity. Yet it is beyond reasonable doubt that Jesus knew he was to be betrayed and, at this last supper with his friends, even identified the betrayer. As he had foretold, 'the Son of Man is to be betrayed into human hands' (Mark 9:31). Whatever the motivation or immediate cause, that was precisely what was about to happen, and before the night was over.

A reflection

Any one of us can be a friend of Jesus, like John—or his betrayer, like Judas. The difference between friend and betrayer may not be very great, especially where human motivations and weaknesses are concerned. What is certain is that Jesus loved them both, knew them through and through and, right to the end, offered both of them a place in his fellowship. The decision was theirs, just as it is ours. In the old military challenge, 'Friend—or foe?'

Day 35: Tuesday

A NEW PASSOVER

READ 1 CORINTHIANS 11:23–26.

Key verse: He took the cup also, after supper, saying, 'This cup is the new covenant in my blood. Do this, as often as you drink it, in remembrance of me' (v. 25).

The Passover meal was under way, even if there was an uneasy, tense air about the proceedings. It was clear that Jesus himself was anxious: 'troubled in spirit' is how John describes it (13:21). It was strange and unsettling to most of the disciples that Judas had suddenly left the company, although some assumed that, as the treasurer of the group, he had simply gone out to pay the landlord. John's Gospel has no account of the meal that followed Judas' departure, but the other Gospels all record the way in which Jesus took the Passover ceremony and dramatically altered its emphasis. Today's passage from Paul's first letter to the Corinthians, written in about AD54, is, by some distance, the earliest account we have of that momentous event.

The meal began in its traditional way, with the table laid out with the finest available tablecloths and napkins, and the dishes, cups and glasses in position. Each participant had a cup for the wine, which was served at four points in the meal—two before the food was served and two after it was eaten. A plate with four large pieces of unleavened bread was at one end of the table, flanked by the candlesticks. On the most impressive dish, the *seder* plate in the centre of the table, there was green herb, bitter herb and *haroset*, made from chopped apples, nuts, cinnamon and wine. Here, shortly, would also be placed the roast lamb.

Jesus started by saying the blessing over the first cup of wine: '*Baruh atah adonai eloiheinu...* Blessed are you, Lord our God, ruler of the universe, creator of the fruit of the vine.' Usually, at this point, a young child of the family would ask, 'What is the meaning of the precepts which God commanded us concerning the Passover?'—to be answered with an account of the deliverance of the Israelites from slavery in Egypt through the power of God alone. On this occasion, we presume, there was no child present, so it would fall to one of the disciples or their leader, Jesus, to speak the yearly reminder of the salvation of the people over a thousand years earlier. This account is always expressed in the present tense, as though each one participating in the Passover had been there during the plagues, on the night of departure and at the crossing of the Red Sea: 'We thank you, Lord our God, for... bringing us out from the land of Egypt and redeeming us from the house of bondage.'

The meal proceeded along its normal course until Jesus took the bread to bless it. In addition to the customary words ('Blessed are you, Lord our God, ruler of the universe, who brings forth bread from the earth'), Jesus surprised and perhaps shocked his hearers by adding some that they had never heard before: 'This is my body that is for you. Do this in remembrance of me' (11:24). He broke the bread and gave it to them to eat. As they took it, they must have wondered at the significance of what he had just said. If the Passover bread, broken before their eyes, was in some way the body of Jesus, that seemed to give him a role similar to that of the sacrificed lamb, also broken on that distant night 'for you', and also to be held in perpetual remembrance.

The meal again progressed in the traditional way until they came to the final cup of wine, the 'cup after supper'. Again Jesus used the usual words of blessing, but then again added some new ones: 'This cup is the new covenant in my blood. Do this, as often as you drink it, in remembrance of me' (v. 25). This was an even more surprising and shocking claim, because Jesus was identifying himself as the agent of a new covenant between God and his people—a covenant sealed with his blood.

The disciples would probably have seen the significance of this concept more clearly than 21st-century Christians do. The relationship between Israel and the Lord God was based on the principle of covenant, a binding agreement between two parties. Abraham, as a reward for his obedience, was given a covenant promise by God that, through his descendants, 'all the families of the earth' would be blessed (Genesis 12:3). Later, at Mount Sinai, after the giving of the law to Moses, God entered into a second covenant with Israel, this time one with a condition. If they would be his people and obey his commandments, he would be their God (Exodus 19:5). The covenant was sealed with the blood of sacrifice—precisely the language Jesus was using about this 'new' covenant, sealed with his own blood.

Suddenly the Passover was transformed. From remembering with thanksgiving a wonderful act of God's salvation in the distant past, they were brought abruptly into the present. Could they really be witnessing the inauguration of a new and even greater covenant, one sealed with the blood of God's own Son? That inevitably would mean the death of Jesus—but then, he'd been speaking about that for weeks and months. Was the moment at hand, perhaps now, during this Passover?

So on the night when 'the Passover lamb had to be sacrificed' (Luke 22:7), Jesus put himself into that very position—as the 'Lamb of God who takes away the sin of the world' (John 1:29). The disciples could not avoid the implications of his words and actions, even if, at that moment, their full significance might be lost on them.

There was a further implication. The 'cup after supper' that Jesus took would presumably have been the fourth and last cup of wine, which meant that it was the 'cup of Elijah'. This was brought in at the end of the meal and set in the middle of the table. After a few seconds of silence, the leader would welcome 'Elijah the prophet, the messenger of final redemption and delivery from all forms of oppression'. The participants would then join in welcoming the prophet, ending with this prayer: 'Elijah the Prophet, Elijah the Tishbite, Elijah the Gileadite—in our own lifetime may he come speedily with the Messiah, the son of David.' We must assume that that was the very cup which Jesus took and gave to his disciples; the very cup with which he sealed the new covenant between God and his new people, the people of the kingdom. It would be hard to think of a more dramatic confirmation of his Messiahship.

Jesus said that they were to do this—break the bread, share the cup—'as often as you eat this bread and drink this cup' (1 Corinthians 11:26). They may have wondered what he meant. Every time they celebrated the Passover ('*this* bread… *this* cup') or every time they ate bread and drank wine? Or—as the first Christians and those who followed after them have generally interpreted it—every time they met together for a meal of thanksgiving? The practice of the first Christians, from the earliest days right through the apostolic era, was clear. They met to break bread frequently, at least once a week, usually on what they called 'the Lord's day', Sunday—and whenever they met in that way, they did it in remembrance of Jesus.

This remembrance was much more than simply remembering him, in the way that we try to remember those who have died in war on Remembrance Sunday. Like the people sharing in the Passover, they were to see that historical event—the death and resurrection of Jesus—as present tense. Although it happened at a place far away, Golgotha, and at a date now far distant in time, those of us who remember Christ in the breaking of bread are bringing that past event into the present, making it part of our thanksgiving and celebration, allowing it to change and shape our lives here and now. We, too, have been brought out of slavery (to self, to sin) and set free. We, too, have left the house of bondage and are on the way to the promised land.

As that unique Passover in the upper room ended and someone started to clear away the dishes, the disciples must have been reflecting on the fact that they had just been involved in an event of eternal significance. There was now a new covenant between God and his people—and they were part of it.

A reflection

Bread and wine were the absolutely staple fare of the people of the day. How remarkable, then, that Jesus chose such simple ingredients for the most widely celebrated meal the world has ever known. The bread of life and the wine of salvation were prepared by human hands, ground and baked in a human kitchen or trodden and bottled in a human vineyard. So Christ decrees that nothing in God's creation is ordinary or mundane. The eye of faith can see the grace of God even, or perhaps especially, in the most common things.

Day 36: Wednesday

A BOLD CLAIM

READ LUKE 22:31–34.

Key verses: And Peter said to Jesus, 'Lord, I am ready to go with you to prison and to death!' Jesus said, 'I tell you, Peter, the cock will not crow this day, until you have denied three times that you know me' (vv. 33–34).

Some of the Twelve remain largely anonymous figures throughout the Gospel records: James the son of Alphaeus, for example, who becomes in later Christian thought 'James the Less', or Bartholomew, not mentioned in John's Gospel but probably to be identified with the Nathanael who met Jesus at the invitation of Philip (John 1:45). On the other hand, enough is recorded about most of the Twelve for them to emerge as rounded and credible figures: the fiery James and John ('sons of thunder'), the questioning, sceptical Thomas, the thoughtful Philip… and Simon Peter, nicknamed by Jesus 'Rock' or, as we might say, 'Rocky'.

Peter was the sort of person who can't stand long embarrassing silences and in that, at least, many of us can probably identify with him. The poor man always felt constrained to say something, however daft it was—like the suggestion about erecting tents for the patriarchs and Jesus on the Mount of the Transfiguration. He saw himself (and seems to have been regarded by Jesus) as the leader of the apostolic band and probably exhibited many of the natural gifts of the leader. He was also impetuous, prone to speak first and think afterwards, unwisely hasty in action from time to time, and far too sure of himself. Even leaders need a touch of self-doubt occasionally, but Peter seemed to lack it completely.

We have thought about the mood of the disciples in the upper room—a mood of excitement mingled with apprehension. That apprehension would have been increased by the sudden exit of Judas Iscariot and then reinforced by what Jesus went on to say: 'Little children, I am with you only a little longer. You will look for me, and as I said to the Jews so now I say to you. "Where I am going. you cannot come"' (John 13:33). Peter could not let this pass, possibly putting into words what all of them wanted to know: 'Lord, where are you going?' (v. 36).

The answer would not have reassured them: 'Where I am going, you cannot follow me now; but you will follow afterwards.' They had all depended totally on the leadership of Jesus since the moment the group came into being: indeed, it was his leadership, and at times that alone, which had kept them together. To face separation from him, even temporarily and especially at this moment of high anxiety, was more than they could bear.

Peter typically put it in personal and unequivocal terms. 'Lord, why can I not follow you now? I will lay down my life for you' (v. 37). It was a splendid and unreserved expression of total commitment, and there is no reason to doubt that, as he said it, Peter meant every single word. He knew his love for and devotion to Jesus but, sadly, he didn't yet know himself. The words were the easy part. Jesus, who knew what lay ahead, could see how deeply his followers would be put to the test and how, at that stage of his discipleship, Peter would fail. There was no way of putting it gently.

'Will you lay down your life for me?' Jesus said. 'Very truly, I tell you, before the cock crows, you will have denied me three times' (v. 38). In other words, that very night would not pass before the bold, brave fisherman Peter would deny knowledge of Jesus. Far from laying down his life for Jesus, he would not even resist the gentle teasing of a servant-girl about his relationship to him and his followers.

Mark's Gospel, possibly reflecting Peter's own recollection of this critical moment, adds a little more detail. Jesus had said that they would all become deserters from his cause, to which Peter retorted that 'even though all [presumably he meant 'all the rest'] become deserters, I will not' (14:29). It was this that provoked Jesus to the statement that 'this very night, before the cock crows twice' Peter would deny him three times. The apostle would have none of it, however. Speaking 'vehemently', he rejected the warning: 'Even though I must die with you, I will not deny you' (v. 31). Significantly, Mark's account adds, 'And all of them said the same' (v. 31): none of them would desert Jesus in his hour of need.

The differences in detail between the various accounts of this incident are fascinating in what they tell us about Peter's place in the early Church, even though they are trivial in terms of the factual record. All of them record the vehemence of Peter's assertion of loyalty and the humiliation of his later denial, though only Mark tells us that it was reinforced with an oath (14:71). In different ways they all also point to the generosity of the forgiveness and restoration to leadership that followed (see, for example, John 21:17). Each Gospel records that Peter swore he would neither deny nor desert Jesus, and Jesus warned him that within a few short hours, before dawn (cockcrow), his boasting would be proved to be empty.

That would not, of course, be the end of the story. In fact, Jesus had already indicated the longer-term outcome of this strange process of protestation and denial. 'Simon, Simon, listen! Satan has demanded to sift all of you like wheat, but I have prayed for you that your own faith may not fail; and you, when once you have turned back, strengthen your brothers' (Luke 22:31–32). The pronouns are important here: all of the disciples were to be 'sifted' ('you' is plural) but Jesus has prayed that Peter's faith (the 'you' and 'your' here are singular) will not fail, although he will need to 'turn back' before he will be in a position to 'strengthen his brothers'. Peter would deny Jesus and, with the others, desert him in his hour of need, but his vocation remained, as would theirs. They had been chosen to be Christ's witnesses and the chastening experience they were to undergo would, in the long run, strengthen rather than weaken that witness.

As for Peter, the even more shaming nature of his denial would, in some strange way, equip him well for future leadership. If leaders need a degree of self-doubt, perhaps they also need a degree of self-awareness. None of his fellow apostles would ever again ascribe to Peter moral or emotional infallibility but, as the subsequent history of the early Church shows, that did not at all disqualify him from a position of sanctified leadership within it. Peter would know himself better and understand the purposes of God better. Equipped with that knowledge, the big fisherman could become the great apostle.

A reflection

To know myself and my weaknesses, and to know Christ and his grace: could these be the twin clues to true discipleship?

Day 37: Thursday

THE PLACE OF PRAYER

READ MARK 14:32–41.

Key verse: 'Abba, Father, for you all things are possible; remove this cup from me; yet, not what I want, but what you want'
(v. 36).

From the upper room, Jesus and the disciples probably made their way through the temple courts, across the Kidron valley and then up the path towards the Mount of Olives. There they came to a garden, one that Jesus had obviously used before as a place of prayer. It was called Gethsemane, which means 'wine press', and it was more like an orchard than a garden, filled with olive trees. It still is today, as many a pilgrim to Jerusalem can testify.

It had been a strange evening, which the eleven disciples would certainly never forget. This had been a Passover meal like no other they had experienced, and now they had made their way from the warmth of the room through the fresh, cool air of an April evening to this lonely venue. Unusually, Mark has the fullest account of what happened there, with several details not recorded in the other Gospels. He notes that when they arrived Jesus seemed 'distressed and agitated' (v. 33)—'deeply grieved, even to death' (v. 34). The quiet garden at this late hour was to be the scene of one of the most heart-rending prayers ever uttered, one of the most shocking betrayals and one of the most cowardly mass desertions in the history of religion. Here was a place of high drama indeed, a moment in which we can see the horror of Jesus the man struggling with the destiny of Jesus the Son of God.

When they arrived, Jesus suggested to the rest of the disciples that they spent time in prayer while he himself moved on a little way into the trees with Peter, James and John. It was with them that he shared his own state of mind, his spiritual turmoil and agitation. Then, asking them to stay awake and pray, he moved on a further few paces and threw himself on the ground, a position identified with the most intense kind of intercession. The subject of his prayer is summarized by Mark in disarmingly simple words: he 'prayed that, if it were possible, the hour might pass from him' (v. 35). This 'hour' was the simplest available Greek word for 'time', yet one that could also carry the meaning of a due time or a moment of destiny.

For weeks and weeks Jesus had been speaking of this moment to his disciples: 'We are going up to Jerusalem, and the Son of Man will be handed over to the chief priests and the scribes, and they will condemn him to death' (Mark 10:33). Yet now that the hour had arrived, it was Jesus who was distressed and agitated, rather than the anxious disciples. He had painted the coming scene for them so vividly that it must have come as something of a shock to Peter, James and John that the imminence of the foretold event could prove so deeply disturbing to him. He had walked boldly ahead of them to Jerusalem, confident, it seemed, in the divine purpose that drove him on. After all, he had told them that the Son of Man 'must' undergo great suffering and be killed (8:31)— indeed, that this was God's purpose, out of which would come blessing. Why, then, did he now shrink from it?

Jesus' prayer continued, presumably overheard by the three disciples: 'Abba, Father, for you all things are possible.' They had heard that phrase on his lips before—'for God all things are possible'—but in that earlier situation he had been talking of the possibility that even a rich person might be saved (10:27). Here, to their astonishment, he was speaking of something infinitely more mysterious, an alteration to the working out of God's purposes through his chosen Messiah. 'Remove this cup from me': the request was simple, at one level. The cup, as the disciples would have known, was the bitter cup of suffering—even, perhaps, the cup that holds the wrath of God against sin (Jeremiah 25:15). But, if everything is possible for God, why couldn't he find a less shameful and brutal way for the world's salvation to be won? Could there not be a less horrible 'plan B'?

There is a tendency for Christians reading the Gospels to view them so exclusively through the lens of the resurrection that they miss the reality of the horror that faced Jesus at this point. We know that he is the Son of God. We know that God raised him from the dead. We know that the suffering and death ahead of him were part of God's purposes of love, the means by which healing and forgiveness would become available to the entire human race. With all that in mind, we might tend to think of Christ's suffering and death as elements in a kind of cosmic drama rather than the actual experiences of a flesh-and-blood man. 'Cheerful he to suffering goes,' says Samuel Crossman's beautiful hymn on the passion ('My song is love unknown'), but it is hard to find cheerfulness in the garden of Gethsemane—nor should we expect to.

Jesus of Nazareth was fully human. It would be a grievous misunderstanding of the incarnation if it were not so. The Son of Man was also, of course, the Son of God: that is the clear teaching of the New Testament. In him the two natures were both fully present. As a man, Jesus looked at what lay ahead and was appalled. His body would be assaulted, scourged and beaten. Nails would be driven through his wrists. As he hung on the cross, his internal organs would be ruptured. Finally, in the heat of the afternoon, he would die. All of this horror would be witnessed by his mother and his friends, while he himself would feel abandoned by his heavenly Father. It's hard to see anything in that prospect to evoke cheerfulness.

Yet because he was also the Son of God, the prayer in the garden didn't end there. It went on, 'Yet, not what I want, but what you want' (Mark 14:36). Even in the face of the most appalling suffering, rejection and death, with all the mysterious consequences of dying for the sins of the world and the temporary but real severing of the eternal relationship of intimacy with his Father that death would entail, the divine will and purpose that Jesus had set himself to follow remained paramount in his intentions. 'I seek to do not my own will, but the will of him who sent me' (John 5:30): that had been the benchmark of his whole ministry. Now it faced its sternest test, but the Messiah did not fail.

Jesus didn't want to be scourged and beaten, crucified and killed. If that sounds obvious, it probably still needs to be said. If it sounds shocking or even blasphemous, then we have not fully taken on board the meaning of the incarnation. The issue for Jesus in the garden was to set aside his own wishes, fears and feelings as a man, in order to fulfil the will of his Father. Samuel Crossman probably had in mind some words in the letter to the Hebrews when he spoke of Jesus going 'cheerfully' to his death: 'For the sake of the joy that was set before him [he] endured the cross, disregarding its shame' (12:2). In fact, this speaks of the purpose of the suffering—the joy that was set before him outweighing, for Jesus, the unavoidable shame of crucifixion that had to be endured. There in the garden of Gethsemane the struggle was short-lived, because both the Father and the Son knew that the outcome of the suffering would be healing for the nations.

The spiritual test was over. Exhausted—his sweat, Luke tells us, like 'great drops of blood' (22:44)—he went to find his friends in the darkness. Urged to stay awake and pray, at the moment of his greatest need they had fallen asleep.

A reflection

Mark, alone of the Gospel writers, tells us that the prayer of Jesus was addressed to 'Abba', the Aramaic name of intimacy for a father. It was the household name, the name that could be used by children as well as adults, a name that spoke of the precious ties of family and blood. When Jesus cried out in his agony, his prayer was not addressed to a remote creative force or to some implacable and unmovable higher power, but to his 'Father in heaven'. So may ours be, in our moments of agony and sorrow. We can come as children to a loving heavenly Father—Abba.

THE PLACE OF BETRAYAL

READ LUKE 22:47–53.

Key verse: Jesus said to him, 'Judas, is it with a kiss that you are betraying the Son of Man?' (v. 48).

Yawning and dragging themselves to their feet, the disciples tried to respond to the call of Jesus to be ready for the betrayer and his associates. 'Get up,' he said to them, 'and pray that you may not come into the time of trial' (v. 46). Time of trial? This wasn't quite how they had visualized the coming of the kingdom of God. It felt more like the triumph of the kingdom of darkness. In the distance they could see the flare of torches and hear the feet of a crowd of people on the paths. Jesus stood before them calmly, as though he knew exactly what was to happen next, while they grouped themselves around him, not sure what was going on even at that very minute.

When the crowd arrived, the disciples could see, even in the darkness, that it was made up of officers of the temple police and religious elders and that it was led, bizarrely, by their erstwhile fellow disciple, Judas. He approached Jesus to kiss him in greeting, presumably as some kind of signal of identification to the officers, although why so well-known a figure as Jesus needed such identification is not clear. Possibly, in the gloom and shadows of the garden, the arresting party feared that they might grab the wrong man.

Jesus himself stood impassively, making no move to escape or resist arrest. The disciples, however, asked him if now was the time for them to use one of the swords they had earlier shown Jesus in a strange and largely inexplicable conversation (vv. 35–38). It could never have been part of the Messiah's plan that his followers should try to fight the temple authorities with a couple of swords. That would hardly be 'turning the other cheek', which he had earlier advocated as the correct response to injustice: 'Do not resist an evildoer. But if anyone strikes you on the right cheek, turn the other also' (Matthew 5:39).

One of the disciples (Peter, predictably, according to John 18:10) was holding one of the swords and decided that this was the time for action. Wielding it perhaps rather inexpertly, he cut off the ear of the high priest's slave, only for Jesus to rebuke him ('No more of this!' Luke 22:51) and then heal the injured man. Matthew adds some more words of Jesus at this point, words that have echoed down the centuries as the human race has constantly turned on itself in violence and bloodshed: 'Put your sword back into its place,' he said to Peter; 'for all who take the sword will perish by the sword' (Matthew 26:52). He then spoke to the crowd who had come to arrest him: 'Have you come out with swords and clubs as if I were a bandit? When I was with you day after day in the temple, you did not lay hands on me. But this is your hour, and the power of darkness' (Luke 22:52–53).

Light and darkness are themes that run through the Gospels and the teaching of Jesus. The Son of Man represented, indeed embodied, the principles of the kingdom of light. The temple and its leadership represented the principles of the kingdom of darkness. Sooner or later, being on a collision course, there would be a confrontation, but it was not to be a war fought with weapons and decided by force of arms. There in the garden of Gethsemane the two sides faced each other, as they soon would in the palace of the high priest. Superficially it seemed that the overwhelming advantage lay with the status quo, the tired and corrupt establishment. This would be 'their hour, and the power of darkness' (see v. 53). That was how it had to be, in order for the true nature of the new kingdom to be revealed.

We can only guess at the feelings of Judas at that moment. If, as I suggested earlier, he was hoping that a move like this by the temple authorities would provoke Jesus into some kind of instant and dramatic response, he would have been bitterly disappointed. The man who had spoken for many weeks of his coming arrest and crucifixion still seemed to acquiesce in his fate. Surely the Messiah of God would not allow these bogus representatives of the covenant people to have their own way?

Yet that was precisely how it seemed to be. The one little spark of resistance by Peter was condemned by Jesus. Judas would not have known of Christ's agony in the garden, the tears and prayers. All he saw now was the one who had been his teacher and Lord allowing himself to be led away by a motley band of collaborators with the Roman power. For Judas, too, this must have seemed to be the hour of darkness—unless, of course, his sole motivation was the financial payment, the now notorious 30 pieces of silver. According to Matthew, however, when Judas saw that Jesus was being handed over by the chief priests to the secular power, the Roman governor, he 'repented', brought back the 30 pieces of silver—throwing them down in the temple—and told the elders and chief priests that he had betrayed 'innocent blood' (Matthew 27: 3–4). He then went out and hanged himself.

Luke offers a rather different account of Judas' end, with no mention of repentance or suicide, although he is described as 'falling headlong' in the field that had been purchased with the silver pieces (Acts 1:18). The difference between the two stories probably reflects different traditions among the early churches and only illustrates for us the difficulty that Christians have always had in interpreting the character and actions of Judas Iscariot. What is certain, it seems, is that at the moment of the arrest of Jesus he was part of the 'hour of darkness'.

As the temple police led Jesus away, 'all the disciples deserted him and fled' (Matthew 26:56), including a young man (very probably Mark himself) who had an unforgettably embarrassing moment. As he turned to run away, one of the guards caught hold of his loincloth, leaving him to make off into the trees stark naked (Mark 14:51–52). This little incident serves to remind us that it was not only the Twelve (or now, sadly, eleven) who were following Jesus, but a larger group, including women. At this moment of high drama, it seems that their collective nerve broke and they all decided that flight was the best and only option. The lone figure of Jesus was led away from the Mount of Olives towards the gate of the city and the palace of the high priest.

A reflection

When Jesus healed the ear of the high priest's slave, he performed the last healing miracle of his earthly life. There is something very revealing about the character of Jesus, that his last healing touch was for a man who was helping to arrest him, just as his last words of forgiveness were for the thief hanging alongside him on Golgotha.

Day 39: Saturday

FOLLOWING AT A DISTANCE

READ LUKE 22:52–54; 23:49.

Key verse: But Peter was following at a distance (v. 54).

All through the journey from the mountain of the transfiguration to Jerusalem, whatever had happened and whatever he may have said, the disciples kept close to Jesus. The less certain they were about the future direction of events, the more they seemed to need his reassuring presence. We can capture this feeling very powerfully at the meal in the upper room, when Jesus himself was troubled and anxiety began to spread like a mini-plague among the disciples. Jesus clearly sensed their unease, and spoke words of reassurance to them: 'Do not let your hearts be troubled.' ('Set your troubled hearts at rest' is how the New English Bible translates it.) 'Believe in God, believe also in me' (John 14:1). It was a straightforward call to them to trust Jesus as they trusted God himself. Would he have led them this far only to abandon them as 'orphans' (v. 18)?

Yet now, at the moment of his arrest in the garden, that seemed to be exactly what Jesus had done. Surely the man who healed the sick and even raised the dead was not helpless in the face of a couple of dozen members of the temple police? He had called them to follow him, but did that include following him into the hands of the enemies of the true kingdom of God? Whatever spiritual sustenance Jesus received in the garden as he prayed had not been given to them (perhaps largely because they had fallen asleep). Now, as their leader was led away, they felt abandoned, alone, bewildered by events and frightened for their own lives. Not surprisingly, they took the obvious course of action and fled into the darkness.

Their flight did not mean that they had lost their devotion to Jesus, but that their conviction that he was God's Messiah had been put to the sternest possible test. For the moment, they could not square the role of Messiah with the ignominy of arrest by the temple authorities, much less the probability of his crucifixion, about which he had so worryingly spoken to them. How could the Messiah be treated as a common criminal, handed over to the Gentile powers and executed? Where was the kingdom in that?

Several of the disciples, and especially the women, eventually made their way into the city to be near Jesus. Finally they came to Golgotha and watched his crucifixion from a distance. A small group, just three or four, were allowed to stand near the cross, among them three Marys—his mother, the wife of Clopas and Mary Magdalene. With them stood one male disciple, John, described as the disciple Jesus loved.

Peter, we read, 'followed at a distance' (Luke 22:54). Presumably the arresting party, with the prisoner, made their way back to the palace of the high priest for the first of several hearings during the night. Peter, we may assume, waited until they were at a safe distance and then followed, wanting to know what was happening and perhaps hoping against hope that, in some marvellous way, Jesus would turn the tables on his captors. It was not to be, at least not in any way that Peter could conceivably have imagined, but his expedition would take an unexpected and unforgettable turn—one that became a turning point in his own life.

A reflection

To follow at a distance is not a satisfactory option for the Christian disciple. The branches of the vine can't draw sustenance from the tree at a distance. 'I am the vine,' Jesus said, 'you are the branches. Those who abide in me and I in them bear much fruit, because apart from me you can do nothing' (John 15:5). To follow at a distance is to be apart from Jesus, whereas the secret of discipleship is closeness to him. As the ancient prayer of St Richard of Chichester pleads, 'May I see thee more clearly, love thee more dearly and follow thee more nearly, day by day.'

Day 40: Palm Sunday

THE COST OF FOLLOWING

READ LUKE 14:25–30.

Key verse: 'Whoever does not carry the cross and follow me cannot be my disciple' (v. 27).

All through the final weeks of the journey to Jerusalem, Jesus had been teaching and warning his disciples. To follow him was not an easy option, a kind of short cut to glory and power. The larger the crowds who came to hear him, the more determined he seemed to be to show them that to follow the suffering servant of Yahweh was to walk a path through, not around, opposition and misunderstanding. The Twelve heard this message often but, right up to the moment of his betrayal, arrest and crucifixion, they seemed cautiously optimistic that it wouldn't really be like that. Where the wider circle of disciples were concerned, including the faithful women who followed him, we can assume there was a similar reluctance to believe that God's Messiah could possibly be rejected and killed by God's own people.

'Large crowds were travelling with him,' Luke tells us (v. 25), and the very sight of them seems to have stirred Jesus to set out the conditions of discipleship in the same stern terms as he had earlier done with the Twelve (see 9:23–26). If they were to follow him unreservedly (and he was not interested in half-hearted or nominal followers), they would need to understand that that commitment might cause bitterness and separation within their families. If it came to it, they might even have to face a cruel choice between their nearest and dearest on the one hand and the demands of the gospel on the other.

The use of the word 'hate' here by Jesus (v. 26) might, for today's reader, imply that he was instructing them to hate their fathers, mothers, wives and children—and this from the teacher who had told them to love their enemies. In fact, this powerful and dramatic way of making a point—hyperbole—was often used by Jesus, as we have seen, to make a case by deliberate (and obvious) exaggeration. After all, Jesus loved and cared for his own mother and would have fully endorsed the commandment to 'honour your father and your mother' (Exodus 20:12). The point was not to question family loyalties but to establish spiritual priorities.

In this instance, Jesus clearly wanted to spell out as powerfully as he could that to follow him was no light commitment, but meant the dedication of body, mind and spirit to the message and mission of the kingdom. It might, he said, even cost them their lives. To follow him was about 'carrying a cross' (Luke 14:27)— becoming, if necessary, an object of public ridicule and shame.

After all, he told them, it is only wise to make sure before embarking on an important enterprise—building a tower, waging a war—that you can carry it through to its completion (v. 28). Jesus did not want fair-weather followers, and the moment of desertion by the closest of his disciples in the garden of Gethsemane is a reminder that even the truest and best ones were to find the course desperately hard at times. Over the history of the Christian Church, there have been long periods (we are perhaps coming out of one such in the West just now) when the Church expected to be honoured and respected by everyone, its leaders sitting in seats of power and much of its membership nominal rather than deeply committed. The world would never have been turned upside down by a Church like that!

A reflection

On this Palm Sunday, when we remember the crowds that cheered Jesus as he arrived in Jerusalem, it might be salutary to wonder where they were when he was being led through the streets of the same city, stumbling under the weight of a cross. In the upper room after the resurrection, there were, Luke tells us, a mere 120 disciples who had remained faithful (Acts 1:15). It is an astonishing tribute to the power of the Holy Spirit and the truth of the gospel message that from that small group grew the worldwide Christian Church of today. They were the ones who had counted the cost, but still followed him.

Part Four

TRAGEDY— AND TRIUMPH

THE CLAIM PUT
TO THE TEST

READ LUKE 22:55–62.

Key verse: The Lord turned and looked at Peter. Then Peter remembered the word of the Lord, how he had said to him, 'Before the cock crows today, you will deny me three times' (v. 61).

In the upper room, as we have seen, Peter protested that he was ready even to die for Jesus. In the garden of Gethsemane, he claimed that, although all the others might desert Jesus in his hour of need, he never would. It's unkind but true to say that Peter was very good at talking the talk. It's not clear whether or not he really took on board the stern warning that before the next dawn he would deny knowing Jesus but, if he did, it was not enough to prevent him actually doing it.

We must give Peter credit where it is due, however. Most of the disciples fled into the darkness, Peter among them, but he couldn't simply leave Jesus to his fate. As we have seen, he followed behind, keeping discreetly out of sight but making his way towards the house of the high priest, where Jesus was to be put under examination. When he got there, a crowd had gathered, rumours of the arrest of the Galilean prophet having reached the ears of the supporters of the temple party. In the middle of the open courtyard there was a brazier and, in the cool of an April night in Jerusalem, it was a welcome sight. Peter made his way towards it and sat down with a number of others to warm his hands.

He probably hoped that no one would recognize him in the darkness. After all, he had only been in the city a few days, and public attention had been focused on Jesus rather than his followers. To Peter's consternation, however, his cover was almost immediately blown. A servant-girl saw his features in the light from the flames of the brazier and recognized his Galilean accent. 'This man was one of his followers,' she said. Everybody turned to look at him.

Peter felt trapped. He had hoped to be an anonymous observer. He hadn't planned to expose himself to the risk of being arrested as a co-conspirator with Jesus. Whether it was simply fear, embarrassment or even a panic-stricken reaction to an unexpected development, Peter blurted out, 'Woman, I do not know him' (v. 57). Probably unconvinced, the servant-girl moved away, but another person in the crowd—according to John 18:26, a relative of the man whose ear Peter had cut off—pursued the subject. 'I saw you in the garden with him,' he said. Again Peter rejected the accusation curtly.

For a while, the crowd around the fire let the matter drop, probably to Peter's great relief. An hour or so later, however, a man who had been listening to the conversation started it up again: 'This man definitely was with Jesus—he's a Galilean, just listen to his accent' (see Luke 22:59). Peter tried to ignore him but the man was persistent: 'He's one of them!'

At this point Peter seems to have lost all control. Mark, who usually reflects most closely the great apostle's recollection of events, tells us that Peter began to curse and swore on oath that he didn't even know Jesus (14:71). At that moment, while he was still speaking, the cock crowed. For some reason, Jesus was within sight of Peter, perhaps waiting under guard to be taken into the office of the high priest. Luke tells us that 'the Lord turned and looked at Peter' (22:61), and instantly Peter remembered the warning he had been given the previous evening—a warning he had so comprehensively ignored. The cock had crowed and he had denied Jesus.

A comparison of the Gospel accounts of this incident reveals some confusion over exactly how many cockcrows Jesus had predicted and how many took place that morning. What is clear is that the denial by Peter was threefold, as Jesus had predicted (v. 34). That is significant because, in Jewish thought, a statement made three times was legally sealed. A divorce, for instance, could be effected by the husband saying three times over, 'I divorce you.' The failure of Peter was absolute and inexcusable, and that is the whole point of the story. Solemnly and formally, as it were, the very disciple who had been the first to confess Jesus as the Messiah of God became the first solemnly and formally to deny that he even knew him. There is something chillingly recognizable about the whole incident. It is frighteningly, appallingly human, to the extent that no one reading it would be inclined to cast the first stone at poor Peter. We have all been there, though perhaps not in such dramatic and critical circumstances.

As the cock crowed and Peter realized what he had done, he went outside and 'wept bitterly' (v. 62).

A reflection

The disciples ran away and deserted Jesus in his hour of need. Peter, one of the inner core of the apostolic group, publicly denied that he knew him. Judas Iscariot, one of the Twelve, betrayed him to the authorities. We may be inclined to comment that with friends like these, who needs enemies? Yet, even as we think it, we feel rebuked and guilty. Have we not, from time to time, deserted Jesus? Have we not, by word or silence, denied that we belong to him, even if literal betrayal has not been part of our experience? If we stand with Peter and the others in our failure and guilt, we can also stand with them in the forgiveness and restoration that Jesus generously gave to all of them—and to Peter very specifically—after his resurrection.

Day 42: Tuesday

BARABBAS AND THE BYSTANDER

READ MARK 15:1–21

Key verse: They compelled a passer-by, who was coming in from the country, to carry his cross (v. 21).

The temple party had a bit of a problem over the arrest of Jesus happening so near to the Passover sabbath. They wanted him put to death but they also wanted to avoid a public riot or any kind of disorder because that would give Pilate, the Roman prefect (governor) of Judea, an ideal excuse to limit their powers still further. They also needed to get the whole thing over before the eve of the sabbath (sunset on Friday is the start of the sabbath day) because the only alternative would be to have Jesus under detention throughout the festival, with possibilities once again of disorder. For religious reasons, the bodies of the dead would need to be buried before the sabbath, and this also pointed to the need for haste.

All of this helps to explain the unseemly spectacle of all-night hearings before various authorities that the Gospels report. The high priest and his associates questioned Jesus first, hearing much obviously false testimony—some of it contradictory, probably from hired 'witnesses'. Their efforts would have been fruitless (it would have been pointless to take Jesus to Pilate without some coherent charge to lay against him) had he not truthfully answered a final question from the high priest himself: 'Are you the Messiah, the Son of the Blessed One?' (Mark 14:61).

Jesus could not deny his true status, nor would he have wished to evade so direct a question. Nevertheless, his answer was categorical and, as he must have known, deeply provocative: 'I am; and "you will see the Son of Man seated at the right hand of the Power", and "coming with the clouds of heaven"' (v. 62). The high priest would doubtless have made the connection with a passage in the book of Daniel (7:13–14), which goes on to say that the Almighty gave to this 'Son of Man' enormous authority and power so that 'all peoples, nations, and languages should serve him'— and that 'his kingship is one that shall never be destroyed'. It isn't surprising that at this the high priest tore his robes and shouted, 'You have heard his blasphemy!' (Mark 14:64). It would not be blasphemy, of course, if it were true, but the high priest was prepared to overlook that possibility in the light of some kind of a claim by Jesus to kingly power. Surely here was the ammunition they needed to bring him to Pilate on a charge of sedition. 'What is your decision?' he asked the priests, elders and scribes. They all, Mark reports, condemned him as deserving of death. Some went further, he says, and spat on him and struck him (v. 65).

As a result of this night-time meeting, Jesus was held until the following morning and then taken off to Pilate, because only the governor could sanction an execution. The hearing before Pilate was less colourful but led to the same result. The governor questioned Jesus about his alleged claim to be 'the King of the Jews', but received only an ambiguous answer: 'You say so' (15:2). After that, he did not answer any more questions, so that Pilate was 'amazed' (v. 5). Perhaps for that reason or, more probably, for fear of a riot, he seemed to be searching for a way to deal with Jesus that didn't involve his execution.

Apparently, at Passover Pilate used to release one prisoner at the request of the people. On this occasion he had two allegedly political prisoners: a violent rebel against the Romans called Barabbas and the 'king of the Jews', Jesus. There is no record in secular history of this rather strange tradition, which may well have been a local arrangement instigated by the governor for his own purposes. He proposed to the crowd around his palace that either Jesus or Barabbas should be released, and that they could choose.

Matthew 27:16 gives the full name of the other prisoner as Jesus Barabbas, which would mean that the crowd was being invited to choose between two Jesuses, two 'saviours' (for that is what the name means)—Jesus Barabbas or Jesus of Nazareth. Stirred up by the priests and scribes, the crowd screamed for Barabbas. Pilate then asked the crowd what they wanted him to do with 'the man you call the King of the Jews' (Mark 15:12). This time they shouted back, 'Crucify him!' 'Why, what evil has he done?' asked Pilate. They simply shouted back even more loudly, 'Crucify him!' (vv. 13–14).

As Mark tells it, 'Pilate, wishing to satisfy the crowd, released Barabbas for them; and after flogging Jesus, he handed him over to be crucified' (v. 15). It is a sad epitaph to the memory of the man appointed to uphold the law of Rome in Jerusalem that the voice of a hired gang of demonstrators prevailed. Perhaps not surprisingly, Pilate, who had already incurred the displeasure of his masters in Rome, was recalled by them a few years later and dismissed for cruelty.

There follows the most stark of all the Gospel accounts of the passion and death of Jesus. It is as though Mark wants his readers to see that this was no divinely stage-managed performance. Jesus died a real death for real sin, the sin of the world, and the cost was pain, sweat and blood.

First he had to endure the ritual taunting of the prisoner by the execution squad of soldiers. They had heard that this fellow claimed to be some sort of a king, so they dressed him up in mock royal finery—a purple cloak and crown of thorns. Then they offered him mock obeisance, saluting him and saying, 'Hail, King of the Jews' before striking him and spitting on him. Having had their bit of fun, they then led him out on to the narrow street that led through the city and out towards the little skull-shaped hill beyond the walls.

That hill—Golgotha ('Place of the skull' in Aramaic) or Calvary (from Latin *calvaria*, meaning skull)—was, as its name suggests, shaped like a skull. The first-century place of execution is now probably buried underneath the church of the Holy Sepulchre, where tourists are taken to a low cave in the rock which could have been the place of the burial of Jesus. To get a better idea of what it probably looked like, visitors to Jerusalem might prefer to look at what is known as 'Gordon's Calvary'—a rocky outcrop beyond the modern city walls, near the Damascus gate and the bus station. The first-century wall was sited well within the present one, so the present location of the church of the Holy Sepulchre (and hence of Golgotha) would have been outside the city limits. This fits John's claim that the execution party went 'out' to the Place of the Skull (19:17), and the belief in the early Church that the sacrifice of Jesus took place 'outside the camp', like the sacrifices of ancient Israel (Hebrews 13:13).

As the execution party made its way through the narrow streets, the soldiers may have realized that they had beaten Jesus so badly that he couldn't, as was customary, carry his own cross (it was the crossbeam that the prisoner bore, probably on his shoulders). Looking around for a handy substitute, they chose, presumably at random, a man from Cyrene in north Africa, almost certainly a Jew visiting the city for the Passover. Mark calls him a 'passer-by' (15:21); we might equally well call him a bystander. He had come to watch the drama, not to become part of it. When Roman soldiers told you to do something, however, it was wise to obey, so the bystander dutifully took up the cross, placed it on his shoulders and carried it behind Jesus to Golgotha.

The bystander is given a name in the Gospels: Simon. Mark alone adds that he was 'the father of Alexander and Rufus'. That little detail probably reveals more than is immediately apparent. How, for instance, did Mark know it? Who were Alexander and Rufus, named as though his readers would recognize them? Could this Rufus be the man of the same name identified by Paul in his letter to the Romans (16:13) and described as 'chosen in the Lord'?

If (as tradition and some hints in the New Testament suggest) Mark joined Paul in Rome, that might explain how he knew the identity of the sons of Simon of Cyrene. The implication of that, of course, is that the experience of following Jesus on the *via dolorosa*, the path of sorrows, and watching his crucifixion led in some way to Simon's conversion and subsequently of his wife and sons. If so, Simon would not be the first person to set out to observe Christ from a distance but find himself drawn irresistibly into faith in him.

Mark 15 gives the time of the actual crucifixion as nine o'clock in the morning (v. 25), although John places the final verdict of Pilate much later, at 'about noon' (19:14). There seems to be general agreement that from noon onwards the sun faded and the city was shrouded in darkness, and that Jesus died at three o'clock (the ninth hour of the day in the current chronology). Mark's timing seems the more likely, unless Jesus died unusually quickly. Grimly, the whole point of crucifixion as a method of execution was its infliction of protracted pain on the criminal. Six hours in the slowly increasing heat of an eastern day would be more likely to achieve that end than three hours, even in the heat of the afternoon.

At any rate, Mark offers a grim picture of the passion of Jesus. He rejected the probably kindly meant offer of wine mixed with myrrh, a primitive form of pain relief. He uttered no words of forgiveness from the cross; there was no penitent thief, just a loud cry of utter dereliction from the lips of the Messiah: 'My God! My God! Why have you forsaken me?' (v. 34). The chief priests and scribes shouted mocking words, inviting the Messiah to come down from the cross and save himself. Meanwhile, the soldiers sat under the cross, waiting for the inevitable moment of death when their miserable duty would be done.

Barabbas and Simon of Cyrene presumably went their separate ways, Barabbas to formulate further plans to overthrow the Gentile usurpers with force of arms, Simon to tell his family what had happened and the impact that that stumbling, bleeding figure had had on him.

A reflection

People are constantly faced with a choice between the two 'saviours', Barabbas and Jesus of Nazareth. It is the choice between worldly power and spiritual authority, between war and peace, between violence and forgiveness, between the way of the sword and the way of the cross. One is built on the expectation of success, the other on the necessity of sacrifice. The way of the cross, as Simon of Cyrene must have seen, is painful, hard and costly, but in the end it leads to life.

Day 43: Wednesday

THE PENITENT THIEF

READ LUKE 23:39–43.

Key verse: He said, 'Jesus, remember me when you come into your kingdom' (v. 42).

It's not surprising that the pictures of the crucifixion offered to us by the Gospel writers vary, though more in emphasis and detail than in substance. If Matthew is looking at it through Jewish eyes—or perhaps, more specifically, the eyes of Jewish converts to Christianity—it's not surprising that he gives a great deal of attention to the words and actions of the high priest, the Sanhedrin and the temple followers who gathered to mock Jesus on the cross. From the very opening of his Gospel, Mark is looking for signs of the final conflict between light and darkness. John, from a more detached perspective, is reflecting a picture of Jesus as the ultimate victor, even in moments of apparent humiliation. His final words from the cross (John 19:30) are a shout of triumph: 'Accomplished!' meaning 'I have finished the work you gave me to do.' That's a long way from the cry of dereliction recorded by Mark (15:34).

Luke may well have had access to the memories of Mary the mother of Jesus, who watched the appalling spectacle from the foot of the cross. If so, he could be recording some things that would not have been visible or audible to people standing at a distance. This may account for two of the most memorable moments of the passion of Jesus, moments that seem to capture something distinctive, possibly unique, about his attitude to human sin and failure.

The first relates to the band of soldiers who were, at that very moment, engaged in putting him to death. As he was nailed to the cross, Luke records, Jesus prayed for them: 'Father, forgive them; they do not know what they are doing' (23:34). It needn't worry us that some translations, including the NRSV, have a footnote recording that 'some ancient authorities' lack this verse. After all, it is present in the book because the weight of textual evidence supports its inclusion. Not only that, but we can be sure that in times when the Church was under violent persecution from the Roman authorities (a persecution that began at about the same time as this Gospel first saw the light of day) this would not have been a popular prayer automatically echoed by its members. The fact that it was included bears testimony to its authenticity. The early Church recognized it as exactly the kind of prayer that the Jesus they knew and revered would have prayed in those circumstances—and it was echoed by the Church's first martyr, Stephen, as he died under a hail of rocks (Acts 7:60).

Jesus died so that sins might be forgiven. Here, with that death only a few hours away, he forgives a sin of ignorance rather than malice. Perhaps it was this very prayer that helped to convince the centurion in charge of the troop of soldiers that the man they were executing was 'innocent' or 'righteous' (Luke 23:47).

The second incident that is unique to Luke is the story of the penitent thief. The Gospels agree that two criminals were executed alongside Jesus and that either both or one of them poured scorn on his situation: he had claimed he was a king, yet he was as helpless as they were. Matthew 27:44 and Mark 15:32 put it in very simple words: 'they taunted him'.

Luke, however, has a different insight into the behaviour of the two thieves. The only possible sources of this information for him would have been John or Mary the mother of Jesus, who were near enough to the cross to hear what was said (see John 19:25–26). They must have passed on to Luke the astonishing encounter between a condemned thief and the Messiah.

One of the criminals was taunting Jesus by suggesting that if he were the Messiah he could save himself from the cross and, while he was about it, save them as well. This was in line with the shouts of derision from the watching scribes and elders. The other criminal, however, must have detected something special about the man hanging next to him, the man named by the accusation over his head as 'Jesus of Nazareth, king of the Jews' (Luke 23:38).

Two things in that description probably caught the attention of the condemned and dying man. The first would have been the ascription of kingly power, unqualified by any such phrase as 'he claimed to be...' or 'the false king of the Jews'. That was the kind of accusation the priests had wanted Pilate to authorize, but he had curtly dismissed their suggestion with the cutting phrase (even briefer in Greek than it is in English), 'What I have written I have written' (John 19:22). So there it was, over the head of Jesus.

Secondly, the thief may have noticed the name 'Jesus of Nazareth'. It's unlikely that the healer and miracle worker from Galilee was totally unknown even among the criminal fraternity. He and his co-criminal were obviously Jews (or why the reference to the Messiah?) and therefore would have known that the name Jesus—*Yeshua* in Hebrew—meant 'saviour' or 'deliverer'.

Whatever the reason, this man saw things very differently from the taunting one on the other side of Christ. He rebuked his scornful words. 'Have you no fear of God, since you are under the same sentence of death as he is?' he asked, in effect. 'The difference is, we have been condemned according to the law, but this man has done nothing wrong' (Luke 23:40–41). He then addressed the figure on the central cross. 'Jesus,' he said, 'remember me when you come into your kingdom' (v. 42).

It is amazing but true that the thief on the cross is the only person in the whole of the Gospels who is recorded as addressing Jesus by his name. For all the others, it is Master, Teacher or Rabbi—but never the name he would have been called by his father and mother in Nazareth or by the children he played with in the streets there. He added, however, an expression of faith in Jesus as the true king of the kingdom that was to come: 'Remember me when you come into your kingdom.' When the crucified Saviour returns in his kingly power, the thief is saying, will he spare a thought for this poor condemned man who called to him from the brink of his own death? He didn't ask much—just to be 'remembered', borne in mind, when that great Day of the Lord came. As an expression of humble repentance and simple faith, it's hard to beat the words of this desperate condemned man.

Jesus responds as anyone who has read the Gospels up to this point would expect, though with a surprising degree of unreserved welcome. 'Truly'—the typical *amen* with which Jesus often preceded a statement of particular significance—'Truly I tell you, today you will be with me in Paradise' (v. 43). Not at some unknown date of the future coming of God's kingdom; not on the day when the throne of David is restored and the new reign of righteousness begins; not then but now, today, the thief is promised to be with Jesus in 'Paradise'. This is not at all the usual word for 'heaven'. In fact, it is both more and less than that. 'Paradise' (this is the only use of the word in the entire Bible) was, in ancient thought, a walled garden of sheer delight—Eden, if you like. Some people could be admitted as companions of the owner, with the right to stroll there and enjoy it. In Jewish thought at the time of Jesus, Paradise was a place of rest and refreshment where people awaited resurrection—which gives added meaning to the promise that the thief would be 'with me' in Paradise. This, then, was a promise that the penitent thief would go from his hideous death on the cross to a garden of delight and that Jesus himself would be there. Beyond that lay the wonderful hope of the resurrection, which he could confidently anticipate in the light of his total acceptance by the Saviour.

Luke has a special place throughout his Gospel for those whom the world despised. In the culture of his time, they included Samaritans, Gentiles, slaves, lepers and, as it happens, women. It is somehow doubly fitting that the last two people in his Gospel who found signs of hope and goodness even in Jesus' death were this miserable criminal and the Gentile officer in charge of the squad executing him.

A reflection

The thief on the cross should remind us that it is never too late to turn to Christ—and we should not despise 'deathbed conversions'. This man's plea for mercy has all the hallmarks of sincerity, and the response of Jesus is instant, complete and affirming. The request was simply for 'remembrance'; the gift given was nothing less than redemption.

THE SPECTATORS

READ LUKE 23:44–49.

Key verse: When all the crowds who had gathered there for this spectacle saw what had taken place, they returned home, beating their breasts (v. 48).

It had been a long journey and it ended here. That's what Peter and John, from their different vantage points, must have thought as they watched the scene on the rocky outcrop known locally as the Place of the Skull. It had been a long journey from the shores of Galilee, the boats and the fish. It had been a long journey through the villages and little towns around the lake—a wonderful journey, full of miracles and healings and wise teaching. It had been a long journey from the hilly north, around Caesarea Philippi, down the Jordan valley and then up to the city of God, Jerusalem, with its markets, street stalls, palaces and magnificent temple. It had been a long way, and it ended here, under a mournful sky, with shouts and cries and bleeding hands and swearing soldiers. Was this the intended destination?

Executions were public affairs and always drew large crowds of onlookers. This time, the crowds may have been bigger than usual, because the prophet from Nazareth had a reputation and a following, and the temple authorities had drummed up something of a mob to stand around and shout insults at him. Most of the watchers, though, were probably just there for the event, so they could say, 'I was there the day they crucified that Jesus from

Nazareth—you know, the one people thought might be the Messiah.' Some, as we have seen, were there to ensure that the Roman prefect felt supported and affirmed in the miserable choice he had made. A few were those closest to Jesus.

Among them was Simon Peter, called to follow Jesus in Galilee three years earlier and the natural leader, it seemed, of the apostolic group. He always saw himself in that leadership role. He was the first to put into words the disciples' growing belief that Jesus was the Messiah (Mark 8:29). He spoke up in objection to Jesus washing the disciples' feet at the last supper (John 13:8). He swore that even if the others deserted Jesus, he never would (Mark 14:29). When Jesus was arrested, he was the one to offer resistance and cut off the ear of the high priest's slave (John 18:10).

Yet, when the moment came later that night, under questioning from a servant-girl, he had denied, with oaths, that he had anything to do with Jesus. The very memory of it was shameful and Peter couldn't bring himself to stand at the foot of the cross to witness at close quarters the death of the one he had deserted. Instead, he kept his distance and watched from afar with other disciples, men and women.

The Gospels are not entirely of one mind as to where the various associates of Jesus stood to watch the awful event, but John's description of a small inner core of those closest to Jesus, standing at the foot of the cross, has the ring of truth. The next of kin were permitted to watch the execution, which meant that Mary the mother of Jesus was there. John stood beside her, shortly to be charged by the dying man with the responsibility of caring for her in the future. The sad little party by the cross was completed by Mary's sister, another Mary (the wife of Clopas, or Cleopas), and then a third Mary, Magdalene, who seems to have had a particularly intense devotion to the man who had delivered her, at some time in the past, from the power of evil (Luke 8:2).

Of the male disciples there seems little doubt that John was closest to Jesus: he was the 'beloved disciple', in the language of the fourth Gospel. It would seem that Jesus had several close friends, including Lazarus, Mary and Martha, to whose home at Bethany he made frequent retreat, and the inner core of the Twelve, usually named as Peter, James and John. Even among those, however, John appears to have been closest to him, as his 'bosom' friend (to take the more or less literal meaning of John 13:25), and here, at the moment of the Master's greatest need, he is on hand while the other disciples keep a more discreet distance.

It was literally from the cross, in the last hour of his life, that Jesus charged John with responsibility for his mother and also asked Mary to accept John as her son (John 19:26–27). From that day, the Gospel says, John took her into his own home—Mary being a widow, of course, though probably still less than 50 years old. Later, we may assume, they shared a home: tradition suggests that it was at Ephesus.

John had followed Jesus for the same length of time as Peter, having previously been a disciple of John the Baptist. Mary, by contrast, had shared life with Jesus since the moment of his conception. She had borne him as a foetus in the womb, held him in her arms when he was born and laid him to sleep in a manger. She had guided his boyhood and teenage years until, with a wrench, she knew that she must let him go so that he could fulfil what she, more than any other human being, knew to be his divine calling. She hadn't thought it would end like this, though. Perhaps only a mother can begin to comprehend what her thoughts and feelings were as she saw her son, a man in his early 30s, slowly and painfully put to death on a gibbet. Yet she stood there. Nothing could have dragged her away from the dark scene, away from the dying presence of her firstborn son.

There were, as we have seen, other women standing with Mary, and more of them watching at a distance. Not for the first or the last time, it was the women who remained loyal and the men who proved unreliable. Mark tells us that there were many women other than the little group by the cross who had come up to Jerusalem with Jesus, including some who had 'provided for him when he was in Galilee' (15:40–41). These faithful women were certainly among his disciples and presumably, also, some of them were to be found in the ranks of the first Christian believers after the resurrection and Pentecost. For now, though, they had simply come out of loyalty and affection to be with their beloved Master in his time of greatest need. After his death, some of them would claim the privilege of carrying out the burial and anointing rites for his body.

So much for those among the spectators at Golgotha who were followers of Jesus. Also standing in the crowd were his professed enemies, including the scornful priests and their miserable mob, chanting insults and ridiculing this powerless and helpless 'king' on the cross. They must have felt it had been a good day's work and, sadly, some of them may even have felt that they were doing what God required, ridding Israel of yet another false prophet and blasphemous 'messiah'.

There were also a few Gentiles present: the small band of Roman soldiers whose duty it was to carry out the executions. For them, this was routine work, crucifixion being the penalty for a wide range of offences, from tax evasion to robbery, violence and inciting anti-Roman feeling—as well as committing murder, of course. Thousands of people in Judea and Galilee had been crucified in the previous 30 or 40 years, often in an attempt to put down local uprisings against the Roman occupiers. So the soldiers would have gone about their task in a routine way—the flogging and ridiculing, followed by the painful procession to the site of execution with the horizontal beam of the cross carried by the prisoner. Then came the assembly of the cross and the strapping or nailing of the criminal to it, before its erection and insertion into prepared sockets in the rocky ground.

Then all they had to do was wait, occupying their time by gambling (for which pastime both archaeology and the Gospels provide evidence: see Matthew 27:35) and ensuring that no one tried to interfere with the execution. Finally, when their centurion had certified that the victims were dead, they would take down the bodies, which would normally be buried in a common grave nearby. Then, their duty ended, they could presumably go back to their quarters for supper. It was, as we say, all in a day's work.

On this occasion, however, there was a difference. Whether the soldiers recognized it or not, we can't tell (although Matthew suggests that they did: see 27:54), but their centurion certainly did. Luke and Matthew say that his response to the death of Jesus was shaped by 'what had taken place'. Mark, intriguingly, suggests that it was the manner of the death of Jesus that impressed the Roman: 'When the centurion, who stood facing him, saw that in this way he breathed his last, he said, "Truly this man was God's Son!"' (15:39). Luke, perhaps more cautiously, puts a slightly less theological interpretation on the centurion's words: 'Certainly this man was innocent [or righteous]' (23:47). In both cases, it is a remarkable tribute from a man who had watched the whole event so closely, observing all that happened and hearing whatever words Jesus spoke from the cross.

One group of spectators remains to be considered and that is the general crowd—the people already mentioned who had come for the gruesome spectacle, like those who used to gather for the public hangings at Newgate or Tyburn in London. They, too, had seen what happened. Perhaps some of them knew a little about Jesus, the prophet from Nazareth. Some might have been inclined to join in the scornful shouts of the temple party; others may have watched out of morbid interest. Some had probably attended many such events—after all, they were common enough on Golgotha.

What did they make of what they had seen, as the soldiers took down the bodies, the eve of Passover drew near and they began to make their way to their homes? Only Luke records the reaction of the ordinary people, but it is further testimony to the awesome nature of what had occurred: 'When all the crowds who had gathered there for this spectacle saw what had taken place, they returned home, beating their breasts' (v. 48). They were not in-different; they were not pleased to see a 'bogus' messiah executed; they were not unmoved by what they had seen. Breast-beating was a sign of grief and repentance—probably not the normal reaction of people who have come to watch the public execution of a criminal.

In the memorable picture that Luke draws for us, there is, of course, desperate sorrow and grief. Mary's heart was surely broken. John watched his dearest friend slowly and painfully put to death. There were darkness and tears and cries of anguish. Also in this scene, however, there is an element of hope for ordinary people. The penitent thief, the grieving crowds and, most surprisingly, the officer in charge of the execution see something special, perhaps unique, in the man whose death they witness. So 'Israel'—the new one—is gathered around the cross. Jew and Gentile together share both grief and hope. As the body is taken down and yet another faithful Jew—a 'member of the council', no less—begs for permission to bury Jesus in a new rock-hewn cave, not in a public pit (vv. 50, 53), it is as though the writer is saying to us, 'The story isn't quite finished yet.'

A reflection

Where might I be among the spectators at the cross? I can't share the particular grief of the mother of Jesus, but do I stand alongside Mary Magdalene, conscious that it was his very death that delivered me from evil? Or with the penitent thief, leaving things to the last minute but turning to a dying Saviour for a promise of hope? With faithful John, perhaps bewildered but simply clinging to his devotion to the man who is also Son of God? Or perhaps with the centurion, not yet fully able to believe but recognizing the marks of divinity even in the death of Jesus? Or simply with the crowd, grief-stricken and guilty? The one on the cross has words of forgiveness and hope for each of us, whoever we are and wherever we stand.

THE TORN VEIL

READ MARK 15:37–38.

Key verse: The curtain of the temple was torn in two, from top to bottom (v. 38).

For all of the Gospel writers, the final act of the drama of Jesus' earthly life was acted out in darkness. This was both physical and spiritual darkness. From noon, the hour of execution, 'darkness came over the whole land... while the sun's light failed' (Luke 23:44–45). It may have been an eclipse, as the Greek word used by Luke suggests, or a duststorm. The spiritual cause is surely more straightforward. The creation itself could not bear the sight of the Creator's Son being put to death. Even the sun hid its face.

There was moral darkness, too: the abuse of power, the rejection of reason, the voices of scorn and hatred aimed at a helpless man on a cross. Soldiers gambled, religious leaders shouted crude insults, innocent bystanders were dragged from the crowd and humiliated—and three human beings had their bodies torn apart slowly and remorselessly under the heat of the dust-laden afternoon.

Yet, in the darkness, each account also records little beacons of hope, indications that perhaps the story was not yet over and that, in the end, light and love and sheer goodness might find a way of conquering darkness and hatred. Some we have already noted: the penitent thief, seeking and finding acceptance and forgiveness at the very point of death; the centurion, recognizing in the dying man proof not of guilt but of innocence; the words of Jesus forgiving the very soldiers who were crucifying him.

John undoubtedly intends his readers to understand that the final cry of Jesus (see 19:30) was also a sign of hope—not an admission of defeat but a claim of victory. 'It is finished' (one four-syllable word in Greek) means 'finished', it is true, but in the sense of 'accomplished' or 'achieved'. It takes us back to the previous evening and the prayer of Jesus just before his betrayal and arrest: 'I glorified you on earth by finishing the work that you gave me to do' (17:4). It may not, at that moment, have looked like 'glory' to Mary and John and the others standing by, yet that is what they eventually realized it was—the glory of a task completed.

The other three Gospels all record another and more symbolic image of hope. Each one reports that as Jesus was crucified (Mark and Matthew place the event at the very moment when he 'breathed his last'), the curtain of the temple was torn in two from top to bottom.

This curtain, or veil, had its origins in the portable tabernacle that was the centre of the Israelites' worship on their wilderness journey from Egypt to the promised land. It separated the Holy of Holies from the Holy Place and only the high priest was ever permitted to pass through it, on the Day of Atonement (see 2 Chronicles 3:14; Leviticus 16:12). When he did, he was bearing in a vessel the blood of a sacrificed bull or ox, which he sprinkled on the altar in atonement for the sins of the people.

The tabernacle signified the earthly presence of Yahweh, the Lord God, whose dwelling was in heaven, and the Holy of Holies was the location at which that presence was to be encountered. It would undoubtedly have been in fear and trembling that the high priest made his way through the curtain once a year, the golden bells on the fringe of his robes letting the people outside know that he was still living and moving even though standing in the awesome presence of the God of heaven. Tradition says that a rope was attached to his ankle, so that in the event of his collapsing or being struck down, those outside could haul him back through the curtain.

Everybody else was kept strictly outside, whatever happened. The only way to God was through the priestly sacrifices. Only through the intercession of the high priest, on his own before God, could the sins of the whole people be forgiven. The curtain was both a barrier and an entrance—a barrier to the ordinary person, an entrance for the anointed high priest.

Now, on a cross on Golgotha, a new high priest was offering a more effective sacrifice to God. Jesus was freely offering himself not just for the sins of a nation but for the sins of the whole world (1 John 2:2). Entrance to the presence of God would no longer be through the intercession of a human high priest bearing the blood of bulls or oxen, but through a new high priest, Jesus the Son of God, offering only (as it were) his own blood. There is no longer a barrier between God and people, only an entrance.

The writer of the letter to the Hebrews puts it in forthright language. He describes the setting up of the tabernacle in the wilderness within a curtain and then goes on:

Behind the second curtain was a tent called the Holy of Holies... The priests go continually into the first tent to carry out their ritual duties; but only the high priest goes into the second, and he but once a year, and not without taking the blood that he offers for himself and for the sins committed unintentionally by the people...

But when Christ came as a high priest of the good things that have come, then through the greater and perfect tent (not made with hands, that is, not of this creation), he entered once for all into the Holy Place, not with the blood of goats and calves, but with his own blood, thus obtaining eternal redemption. For if the blood of goats and bulls, with the sprinkling of the ashes of a heifer, sanctifies those who have been defiled so that their flesh is purified, how much more will the blood of Christ, who through the eternal Spirit offered himself without blemish to God, purify our conscience from dead works to worship the living God!

HEBREWS 9:3, 6–7, 11–14

This is the language of blood sacrifice, which is not much to our taste today, but the concept behind it is a vital one—that sin matters, that it can't simply be airbrushed out of sight. Indeed, it matters so much that only the death of the Son of God could adequately atone for the sins of the world. I have no idea how the principle of forgiveness through sacrifice actually works (although there is no shortage of people ready and willing with a theory to explain it). The truth, however, is almost certainly too great for words and perhaps even for human comprehension. In an act of pue and selfless love, the God of heaven and earth was prepared to submit his Son to a criminal's death so that sins could be forgiven. In the light of that, how could any of us sin lightly or doubt the high price of our redemption?

The Holy of Holies was, in Jewish thought, the place where heaven and earth intersected, where the kingdom of light and love interlocked with the kingdom of frailty and failure, which is human existence without God. Yet it was not a place that people could freely visit. Just one man—and he as frail and fallible as the rest—could go in. The tearing down of the temple curtain on Good Friday symbolized a spiritual revolution. As Tom Wright puts it, 'The place where God's space and our space intersect and interlock is no longer the Temple in Jerusalem. It is Jesus himself' (*Simply Christian*, SPCK, 2006). I suppose that the first place of that 'interlocking' was Golgotha, the Place of the Skull.

That is what makes Good Friday good. There was much that was bad—indescribably so—but carved invisibly in the rock face we can imagine the words, 'God so loved the world that he gave his only Son' (John 3:16). The driving force behind the whole event was not the evil of man, strong and powerful though that can be, but the love of God, which in the end is irresistible.

A reflection

The letter to the Hebrews speaks of Jesus opening a 'new and living way… through the curtain'—a way into the very presence of God. The writer then urges us to 'approach with a true heart in full assurance of faith' (10:20, 22). After all, there's no point in someone opening a door for us if we are not going to enter.

Day 46: Holy Saturday

HE IS NOT HERE!

READ LUKE 24:1–5.

Key verse: 'Why do you look for the living among the dead? He is not here, but has risen' (v. 5).

The disciples didn't simply go home on that sabbath evening. As dusk fell and the women returned from watching the burial of the body of Jesus in a rock-hewn tomb, they seemed to need each other. Bewildered, frightened and anxious, they were not yet ready to write off the whole of the last three years as though they had never happened. It would seem that they made their way to the same upper room where they had eaten the *seder* with Jesus the previous evening. There they shared the emotion and distress of that long Friday. Their leader, their Teacher and Lord, was dead. They had seen his body on the cross. Surely that was not the end of the story? Perhaps they spoke quietly about the mysterious phrase frequently added by Jesus to his prophetic warning about the fate that would befall him in Jerusalem—'and on the third day... rise again' (18:33).

They were aware of the concept of resurrection, which was the belief of most Jews at the time, with the exception of the Sadducees. But they had always thought of it as taking place in the future, associated perhaps with the 'Day of the Lord' or a time of judgment. They had no notion of individual resurrection here and now. The conversation between Jesus and Martha after the death of her brother Lazarus illustrated the contemporary belief very clearly.

Jesus said that her brother would rise again, to which she replied, 'I know that he will rise again in the resurrection on the last day' (John 11:24). With that belief the disciples would have had no problem, but 'three days after being killed, he will rise again' (Mark 9:31)—what could that mean?

Their whole demeanour on that long sabbath day and the next morning tells us that they had no expectation that Jesus would rise from the dead, certainly not there and then. They behaved like men and women who had been bereaved—some anxious to honour him with the simple rites of passage, some numb with despair (think of the two on the road to Emmaus on the Sunday evening) and some torn between a vague hope and a desperate longing. They had seen those tiny signs of hope, of course, but whether or not, at that moment, they were in a state to interpret them is very doubtful.

So it was apparently with no clear hope but with real love and devotion that the faithful women made their way to the tomb the moment the sabbath was over—'at early dawn', says Luke 24:1. They had come to anoint the body of Jesus. All the Gospels tell us that Mary Magdalene was one of them; the identity of her companions varies slightly between the Gospels, but it would seem that there was a party of three or four. As they approached the tomb, they wondered what they could do to roll away the heavy stone that closed the entrance, but in the event they had no need to worry. To their surprise and perhaps consternation, the stone had already been rolled back and the tomb lay open.

They may well have feared the activity of tomb robbers, who were only too ready to pillage tombs that seemed to house the remains of wealthy people. Jesus was not wealthy, of course, but this was a rich man's tomb and so (the women may have feared) a possible target for the robbers. They made their way into the tomb, from the bright light of early morning into the dark interior.

Then came the first shock. Mark gives the briefest and most cautious account of what happened next: 'They saw a young man, dressed in a white robe, sitting on the right side.' Not surprisingly, 'they were alarmed' (16:5). Luke and Matthew describe the young man as an 'angel'—a messenger of the Lord, someone sent to do his bidding. When he spoke, his message was clear, concise and very nearly incredible: 'You are looking for Jesus of Nazareth, who was crucified. He has been raised; he is not here. Look, there is the place they laid him' (Mark 16:6). Luke, for once, is even more concise: 'He is not here, but has risen' (24:6).

Those words are the beginning of the resurrection story. The angelic message had two crystal clear elements. The first was that Jesus was 'not there'—which the disciples could see for themselves: the tomb was empty. The second was the explanation of that emptiness: 'He is risen.' The one who had been crucified, whose dead body the women had escorted to that very tomb on Friday evening, was not there on Sunday morning because he was somewhere else. He was alive—raised by the power of God.

Much was to follow that discovery. Soon they would see him, and that seeing would become the very heart of the apostolic message: 'We have seen the Lord' (John 20:18). Soon the other disciples—'and Peter' (Mark 16:7: what reassurance there must have been in those words for the failed leader of the Twelve)—would see him and know that this was not an hallucination on a grand scale. It had happened.

The women ran off with their message, frightened and excited. As it was passed on, tested and believed, history changed. The life of Jesus had not ended in tragedy and death but in triumph and life. The two greatest enemies of the human race—sin and death—had been faced and overcome. Nothing would ever be quite the same again.

A reflection

I sometimes think it would be nice to erect at the entrance to every graveyard a simple sign with these words on it: 'Not here—risen!' Christians have no need to be grave-watchers, good though it is to have a place to remember with thanksgiving. The tombs are empty and, by the grace of God, heaven is being filled. Whether it is now or at a future day of resurrection will make no difference to those who have slipped away from the confining bonds of earthly time. 'He, or she, is not here, but risen.'

Day 47: Easter Day

THE JOURNEY GOES ON

READ MATTHEW 28:18–20.

Key verse: 'And remember, I am with you always, to the end of the age' (v. 20b).

It had been a long journey from the Mount of Transfiguration to the hill called Golgotha, long and painful. With fear and trepidation, the disciples had followed a Master who had set his face to go to Jerusalem, even though he knew what awaited him there. Over and over again they heard his grimly prophetic words: 'See, we are going up to Jerusalem, and the Son of Man will be handed over... to be mocked and flogged and crucified; and on the third day he will be raised' (Matthew 20:18–19). Now it had all happened, and they were awestruck. Yes, he had been in the hands of those who wanted to have him killed. He had gone through the agony of crucifixion. He had tasted death in its most ugly and vicious form. Then, just as he had said and they had failed to understand, his Father had raised him from death. The tomb was empty. Jesus was alive—and they had met him.

The consequence of Easter morning for the disciples was that the journey was by no means over. There would be a great deal more travelling to do. Of the Twelve, and excluding Judas Iscariot, all but one, it seems, met violent deaths of one kind or another, mostly for refusing to deny that Jesus had risen from the dead. That in itself is the strongest possible argument for its truth: on the whole, people aren't ready to die for what they know is at best a delusion and at worst a lie. They had seen the Lord, and nothing and no one would ever shake that conviction.

Nevertheless, the whole resurrection event was disturbingly traumatic. Mary, the mother of Jesus, would be the chief witness to that. To watch a dear son put to death, to see his body buried—and then, 36 hours later, to sit in an upper room in Jerusalem (we may speculate) and meet him alive again… it all sounds more than a human spirit can comprehend or accept. In a lesser way, all the disciples, men and women, must have gone through the same trauma. It was all over, but suddenly it wasn't. The truth was hard to assimilate: look how the two disciples on the road to Emmaus went through every extreme of human emotion in the course of a seven-mile walk and a brief (and interrupted) meal. Despair, disappointment, grief, confusion, hope, and finally utter, incredulous delight followed in bewildering succession. After the risen Jesus had made himself known to them (as he broke the bread) they ran the seven miles back to Jerusalem, expecting to break the good news to their brothers and sisters in the upper room—only to find that they knew it already (Luke 24:28–35).

The four Gospels seem to be almost as confused as the excited disciples as they try to piece together the momentous events following the resurrection of Jesus. He appeared to the disciples in different ways and in different locations, although Mark, Matthew and John all place his final meetings with them in the place where it had all begun—Galilee. Matthew concludes his Gospel with an account of a kind of recommissioning service on a hillside in Galilee, where he met the Eleven, as they now were.

First he set out for them the unique authority that he, as the risen Son of God, had been given by the Father. In these verses there is a frequent play on the Greek word for 'all': *panta*. All authority had been given to Jesus in heaven and on earth. They were to go under that authority and make disciples of all nations, not simply the lost sheep of the house of Israel on whom Jesus had focused his earthly ministry. They were to baptize them and teach them all that he had commanded them and, as they were doing it, he would be with them 'all the ways they travelled'—the literal meaning of the phrase usually translated in English by the single word 'always'.

It was that continuing presence that would make the journey possible, profitable and fruitful. Two thousand years later, it still is.

A reflection

In one sense, the journey to Jerusalem has no end, because at Jerusalem it led not to completion, but to commission. Having been called by Jesus three years earlier, the disciples were now sent out into the vast, antagonistic, sceptical, suspicious world of the first century.

Armed with faith in the risen Jesus, and shortly to be empowered by the special gift of the Holy Spirit, they turned that world upside down. Within four centuries, belief in the resurrection of Jesus was the received religion of the Roman empire. There were believers in Jesus all over its vast confines and far beyond. Now, two millennia later, the disciples of Jesus are still on the long journey of faith and witness, and the risen Lord, as he promised, is still with them wherever they travel.

DISCUSSION MATERIAL FOR GROUPS

If groups are using this book for Lenten study, it's possible that they will not have their first meeting until the week after the first Sunday in Lent. In that case, the leader may feel that some time should be spent on the vital question raised in the material for Week 1 ('Who is Jesus?'). Similarly, many groups will probably not meet in Holy Week, so the material relating to the crucifixion and the events surrounding it may need to be recognized in the discussions during Week 6.

Each week, a preliminary exercise is suggested—optional, of course, but it may be helpful in involving members who do not usually have much to say and set everyone at ease for the discussion that will follow.

WEEK ONE: SETTING OUT (DAYS 1–4)

Preliminary exercise

Ask a series of light-hearted questions about people's identities and roles: 'Who's Tony Blair? Who's Condoleezza Rice? Who's David Beckham? Who's [name a local or church personality]?' The answers, of course, will tend to describe them in terms of status, position or role. 'Who do people say that I, the Son of Man, am?' is a similar question, and it got a similar answer: 'He's the Messiah.'

Setting out on the journey of faith

It might be interesting to invite people to think about how they came to understand who Jesus is—at what age and whether all at once or over a period of time. For the disciples, their understanding immediately led to a challenge: how seriously do you take this? Then, at the transfiguration, they received confirmation that what they had believed by faith was the truth about Jesus. Can any in the group mirror this experience in any way? In what ways, in our lives, have we become convinced that what we believe by faith is actually true?

For the disciples, the confession of Jesus as Messiah was not the end but the beginning of a long journey of faith. Someone has described confirmation as the church's 'passing out' parade: youngsters are confirmed and then leave! How can we (not only for ourselves, but also for those new in the faith) ensure that the experience of faith becomes the start of a journey rather than the end of it?

Discussing the text

This is an opportunity (perhaps ten minutes: it's wise to set a limit) for people to raise questions, offer their own insights and discuss problems thrown up by the Gospel passages they have been reading. The transfiguration might well raise such questions. (Was it a vision? What was its purpose?) So might the moving story of the epileptic boy and his healing.

WEEK TWO: TRAVELLING LIGHT—AND STUMBLING BLOCKS (DAYS 5–11)

Preliminary exercise

Invite people to describe problems they have had on journeys. Let's have some real horror stories, please—especially any to do with luggage (passenger in Gatwick, bags in Hong Kong) or distractions and stumbling blocks on the way. All of this may illustrate the advantages of travelling light and avoiding snags!

Travelling light and stumbling blocks

What might it mean for Christians today to 'travel light'? We live in a world of 'things': can we do without them? What would be a 'simple' lifestyle for us? Would such a lifestyle be any kind of effective witness to a materialistic world or would we be dismissed as killjoys—and does it matter if we are? If I choose to live simply, can I also insist that my family, especially my children, live simply, too? How could the Christian Church set an example in simple living? Is a simple lifestyle appropriate for the Christian in a world where many have no choice but to live 'simply'?

Are the stumbling blocks on the Christian journey self-inflicted? How can we see the particular stumbling blocks in our own lives? Should we seek the advice of others whom we trust, in case we are blind to them ourselves?

Discussing the text

Questions here may focus on the difficult passage in Matthew 18:8–9. Obviously Jesus wasn't advocating self-mutilation, but drastic problems need drastic remedies—facing up to moral or spiritual weaknesses in our own lives. There might also be questions about the request of James and John. Is ambition always wrong? Is the model of leadership that Jesus offers still valid in today's cut-throat competitive world?

WEEK THREE: SEEING, LISTENING, TRUSTING (DAYS 12–18)

Preliminary exercise

Invite the group to listen to the story of Bartimaeus and then, in five minutes or so of silence, to visualize the scene and place themselves somewhere in it—as one of the crowd, as a disciple or even as Bartimaeus himself. Then people can have the opportunity to share any new insight produced by this reflective experience.

Seeing, listening, trusting

These passages from the Gospels feature several very different characters, each with a different need but all eventually bringing it to Jesus. Zacchaeus needed forgiveness, Bartimaeus needed sight, and Mary and Martha needed comfort in bereavement. People might like to suggest to which character they can best relate and why.

People might also like to discuss the question of missed or taken opportunities, perhaps with instances from their own lives. Both Zacchaeus and Bartimaeus had once-in-a-lifetime opportunities to encounter Jesus, opportunities that they seized. Members of the group may also be able to provide examples of God's patience in coming back to us time and again with opportunities to respond to him—but should we take that patience for granted?

Discussing the text

Again, this is an opportunity for comments, questions, problems and insights that people have brought from the week's readings. Some may be about the rather mystical story of the raising of Lazarus: what does it tell us about Jesus, who describes himself as 'the resurrection'—presumably here and now, rather than at some undisclosed future time? There are themes of 'seeing' and 'listening' in these stories, too, which people may enjoy picking up.

WEEK FOUR: TRUE AND FALSE (DAYS 19–25)

Preliminary exercise

What's the greatest act of generosity you have ever experienced? People may contribute from their own experience and then see if there are any common elements to the stories. (You might be daring and include, for contrast, the most obvious displays of false generosity that people have encountered.)

True and false

During the week, we have read of true and false religion (in the temple, for instance), of true and false discipleship (in those who followed Jesus when he was popular but abandoned him when things got tough) and true and false wealth (in the poor widow compared with the wealthy and ostentatious donors to the temple chests).

How can we tell if religion is true or false? (Is one test persecution? See Mark 13:13). What constitutes true generosity? How do we recognize a true disciple of Jesus?

What would people regard as the things that most put outsiders off the Church? Might they be related to questions of true and false?

Perhaps in a few minutes of silence, people can note on a piece of paper whether they feel that their own discipleship, generosity and religious faith are 'true' or 'false' by Jesus' standards. The pieces of paper can be disposed of, or burnt, after a prayer at the end.

Discussing the text

Most of the discussion about the text would probably centre on the Lord's sayings about the future and the Day of the Lord. It might be best, if this topic is raised, to ensure that the keynote Gospel message is clearly sounded: 'Be alert, because you don't know when.'

WEEK FIVE: FACING THE CHALLENGE (DAYS 26–32)

Preliminary exercise

Ask the group to think of an occasion when each of them felt personally challenged. It doesn't have to be over a faith issue: it might just be failing to complain about a piece of rudeness or unkindness to someone, or even bad service in a shop or restaurant. Why do we find it so hard (or are there some who positively revel in it)? What might we do or say if the circumstances were repeated? (Or what did we wish we'd said or done after it was all over?) The exercise might help to establish why sometimes we ought to speak or act, and also why many of us find it very difficult.

Facing the challenge

The group might like to reflect on the nature of the challenge faced by Jesus and the disciples: the tradition and status of the temple priesthood, the power of imperial Rome, even the vested interests of the traders in the temple courts. It might be helpful to note the way in which Jesus dealt with each of them—recognizing the strength of the opposition but not being silenced or overawed by it, speaking out very boldly at times, and acting in a dramatic and instant way at the corruption of his 'Father's house'.

In our own circumstances, what constitutes the equivalent opposition? People may suggest a variety of ways in which greed, secularism, injustice, moral corruption and so on challenge the Church and its message. How can we best face the opposition? What generally holds us back from open opposition to what we know to be wrong? What could we do to oppose evil without bringing the gospel itself into disrepute?

Discussing the text

Provide an opportunity for members of the group to raise questions or share insights into the text of the passages they have been reading. The dreadful fate of Jerusalem might be one such topic; the significance of Jesus washing his disciples' feet might be another.

WEEK SIX: PUT TO THE TEST (DAYS 33–39)

Preliminary exercise

Try a little dramatic reconstruction! Re-read the story of the betrayal in the garden of Gethsemane, have a short silence and then invite people to identify with one of the characters in the story: the inner core of disciples, who fell asleep instead of keeping awake to pray; Judas, working from whatever tangled motive to identify Jesus to the guards; Peter, lashing out in anger with a sword at one of the guards; the man who was attacked and then instantly healed by Jesus; the other disciples, lurking in the shadows, afraid and appalled at events—even Mark, running away naked. With the scene fresh in people's minds, you could then turn to discussion.

Put to the test

Poor Peter! It would be interesting to find out how members react to his bold words in the garden and his abject denial of Jesus a few hours later. In a sense, most of us deny Jesus from time to time, sometimes by silence, sometimes by inaction—and often under less threat than Peter was. Some people might be prepared to give examples from experience. How do members of the group feel about Peter and, for that matter, about Judas? Do they agree that he could have been Jesus' friend but chose quite deliberately to be his betrayer?

How closely do we feel we follow Jesus? What are the clues to following anybody successfully—a guide, for instance? How can we keep him in sight, hear his voice, follow in his steps, if we are 'following at a distance'?

'Not my will, but yours': how does the group respond to the prayer of Jesus? Have people got examples from their own experience of the challenge of accepting God's will when it clashes with their own (over the outcome of a loved one's illness, for instance, or a job they failed to land)? When we pray for someone or something, should we always add 'If it's your will, Lord', or does that imply a weakness of faith? (The example of Jesus in the garden might be exemplary.)

Discussing the text

Provide an opportunity for people to raise questions or share insights into the passages they have been reading. The institution of the Lord's Supper might raise some questions and offer some interesting reflections, as might the subject of the secret disciples of Jesus. Do secret disciples exist today—and if so, where?

HOLY WEEK : AROUND THE CROSS (DAYS 40–47)

Preliminary exercise

This exercise might well occupy the whole session for a meeting in Holy Week. The passion narrative can be read through again, or the appropriate chapters from this book (Days 42–44, pages 163–179). Then there might be ten minutes or so of silence while people reflect on the scene, especially the characters around the cross and standing at a distance. Members of the group could be invited to identify (if they can and wish) with one or other of the characters, entering as vividly as they can into that person's experience on that day.

The discussion will be the fruit of that reflection, ideally mirroring all the different human reactions to the Saviour, from those of the penitent thief and the centurion to those of Mary, John, Mary Magdalene, Peter and the women standing at a distance. There are also, of course, the enemies of Jesus and the curious (though later subdued) crowd of spectators.

The evening might fittingly end with a hymn (for example, 'When I survey the wondrous cross') and prayer.

Also by David Winter

HOPE IN THE WILDERNESS

BIBLE READINGS FROM ADVENT TO EPIPHANY

'The world has many stories. Some make us laugh, some make us cry, some we forget and others we remember all our lives. But there are a few, very few, that mirror the human experience so vividly and completely that they have themselves become part of that experience. This book retells and reflects on perhaps the greatest of them all, the Exodus—the story of a group of men and women, with a charismatic but flawed leader, making their way from slavery in Egypt to a promised land "flowing with milk and honey".

'It is also a story with profound meaning for many people at the personal level. I began this book while my wife was ill in hospital and completed it in the first year of a painful bereavement. For me it became the story of a slow and arduous journey through a barren and desolate landscape towards a place of distant promise.'

Follow the story with David Winter and discover how we too, like the people of Israel long ago, live under the justice and mercy of God.

ISBN 978 1 84101 258 2   £6.99
Available from your local Christian bookshop or, in case of difficulty, direct from BRF using the order form on page 207.

Also by David Winter

OLD WORDS, NEW LIFE

REFLECTIONS ON 40 KEY OLD TESTAMENT WORDS

While parts of the Old Testament are well known and loved—the poetry of the Psalms, the wisdom of the Proverbs, selected bits of the prophets—other sections tend to remain unexplored, with some readers put off by a general impression of fire and brimstone and excessive violence. To read the New Testament without getting to grips with the Old, however, is like starting a novel in the middle and expecting to understand it properly!

In this book David Winter offers an accessible way of becoming better acquainted with what was, after all, the text that Jesus knew as 'Scripture'. Looking at 40 key words from 'atonement' to 'Yahweh', he provides a Bible passage, helpful explanation and concluding reflection for each one. You can use *Old Words, New Life* as a book for daily Bible study, or as a handy reference tool to check out a particular word that crops up as you are reading the Old Testament.

ISBN 978 1 84101 391 6   £6.99
Available from your local Christian bookshop or, in case of difficulty, direct from BRF using the order form on page 207.

Also from BRF

THE ROAD TO EMMAUS

COMPANIONS FOR THE JOURNEY THROUGH LENT

Helen Julian CSF

Lent is a time when many Christians choose to focus on some of the disciplines of life as a follower of Jesus, from prayer and fasting to Bible study. This book of Lent readings offers us a chance to reflect, day by day, on the experiences and teaching of some key figures in English spiritual history. Through the intervening centuries, their words speak to our hearts, illuminating new truths, enriching our faith and affirming us in our own walk with God.

From a host of possible subjects, author Helen Julian has chosen seven: Julian of Norwich, Thomas Traherne, the Venerable Bede, John Donne, John and Charles Wesley, Aelred of Rievaulx, and the anonymous author of *The Cloud of Unknowing*. She shares something of their stories, their historical context, and the themes unique to their writing. With links to relevant Bible passages, she suggests imaginative exercises for groups and individuals to put into practice what we have learnt.

ISBN 978 1 84101 442 5   £7.99
Available from your local Christian bookshop or, in case of difficulty, direct from BRF using the order form on page 207.

Also from BRF

CHALLENGES OF THE NARROW WAY

BIBLE READINGS AND REFLECTIONS FOR LENT AND EASTER

Bridget Plass

'Enter through the narrow gate; for the gate is wide and the road is easy that leads to destruction, and there are many who take it. For the gate is narrow and the road is hard that leads to life, and there are few who find it' (Matthew 7:13–14). These words of Jesus challenge all who want to follow his way, choosing the path that leads to eternal life.

In *Challenges of the Narrow Way*, Bridget Plass has written a book for Lent that encourages us to face up to the fact that God's calling may not be to a comfortable, successful life, with all emotional and material needs fulfilled. Instead, he calls us simply to follow, taking us on a journey that may be hard, lonely and at times dangerous, but one that leads ultimately to 'treasure in heaven'. And if we acknowledge our weakness, our fear and our sense of unworthiness, he will give us sufficient strength to carry on, every step of the way.

ISBN 978 1 84101 365 7   £7.99
Available from your local Christian bookshop or, in case of difficulty, direct from BRF using the order form on page 207.

ADVENT AND LENT BOOKS FROM BRF

Did you know BRF publishes a new Lent and Advent book each year? All our Lent and Advent books are designed with a daily printed Bible reading, comment and reflection. Some can be used in groups and contain questions which can be used in a study or reading group.

If you would like to be kept in touch with information about our forthcoming Lent or Advent books, please complete the coupon below.

✄--

❏ Please keep me in touch by post with forthcoming Lent or Advent books
❏ Please email me with details about forthcoming Lent or Advent books

Email address: _____

Name _____

Address _____

_____

_____

Postcode _____

Telephone _____

Signature _____

Please send this completed form to:
BRF,
15 The Chambers,
Vineyard,
ABINGDON OX14 3FE

Tel. 01865 319700
Fax. 01865 319701
Email: enquiries@brf.org.uk

www.brf.org.uk

PROMO REF: END/LENT08   *BRF is a Registered Charity*

ORDER FORM

REF	TITLE	PRICE	QTY	TOTAL
258 2	Hope in the Wilderness	£6.99		
391 6	Old Words, New Life	£6.99		
442 5	The Road to Emmaus	£7.99		
365 7	Challenges of the Narrow Way	£7.99		

POSTAGE AND PACKING CHARGES						
Order value	UK	Europe	Surface	Air Mail
£7.00 & under	£1.25	£3.00	£3.50	£5.50
£7.01–£30.00	£2.25	£5.50	£6.50	£10.00
Over £30.00	free	prices on request		

Postage and packing:

Donation:

Total enclosed:

Name _____ Account Number _____

Address _____

_____ Postcode _____

Telephone Number _____ Email _____

Payment by: ❑ Cheque ❑ Mastercard ❑ Visa ❑ Postal Order ❑ Maestro

Card no. ❑❑❑❑ ❑❑❑❑ ❑❑❑❑ ❑❑❑❑

Expires ❑❑ ❑❑ Security code ❑❑❑ Issue no. ❑❑❑

Signature _____ Date _____

All orders must be accompanied by the appropriate payment.

Please send your completed order form to:
BRF, 15 The Chambers, Vineyard, Abingdon OX14 3FE
Tel. 01865 319700 / Fax. 01865 319701 Email: enquiries@brf.org.uk

❑ Please send me further information about BRF publications.

Available from your local Christian bookshop.   BRF is a Registered Charity

Resourcing your spiritual journey

through...

- Bible reading notes
- Books for Advent & Lent
- Books for Bible study and prayer
- Books to resource those working with under 11s in school, church and at home

- Quiet days and retreats
- Training for primary teachers and children's leaders
- Godly Play
- Barnabas RE Days

For more information, visit the **brf** website at **www.brf.org.uk**